UTOPIAS

AND

EDUCATION

by
Howard Ozmon

Burgess Publishing Company

426 South Sixth Street • Minneapolis, Minn. 55415

Educational Consultant to Publisher:
Leo E. Eastman
Head, Department of Education and Psychology,
Illinois State University,
Normal, Illinois

"Without the Utopias of other times, men would still live in caves, miserable and naked."

—*Anatole France*

ACKNOWLEDGMENTS

I wish to thank the staff of the New York City Public Library for their kind assistance in the preparation of this book, as well as the many others who read and commented on it during its various stages of development. I wish to thank The Macmillan Company and Bantam Books for their permission to include selections from previously published material, and I particularly wish to thank Professor Philip Phenix of Teachers College, Columbia University, and Professor James E. McClellan of Temple University, for their invaluable help and advice.

Howard Ozmon

JUL 30 1969

TABLE OF CONTENTS

INTRODUCTION

The term "utopia" is one which has been used in many different ways. Its ambiguousness has resulted from frequent, though not always intelligent, use. It has been used, as More coined the term, to refer to an imaginary island, or as its Greek equivalent implies, a "no where." It has been used disparagingly to refer to the senseless escapist dreamings of those who wish to avoid the realistic construction of a future world. Webster's *New World Dictionary* (College Edition) defines a Utopian not only as one who seeks such an imaginary place, but also as an "impractical" reformer. I have placed "impractical" in quotation marks to point out the negative character of this particular interpretation.

In connection with this, Infield[1] points out that words, like books, have their "social careers," and that some words, like the word "marshal," which originally meant a servant in charge of horses, have risen to a higher status today; whereas a word like "knave," which originally meant young man, has lost its original meaning and stature. He goes on to show that the word "utopia" has also undergone such a metamorphosis. Under the meaning given to it by More, *i.e.,* the picturing of an ideal society with goals man could strive for, it enjoyed an eminent reputation. It was largely due to Karl Marx, Buber[2] believes, that the reputation of "utopia" sank in value. Marx, he argues, used the word as a weapon in the fight between Marxism and non-Marxian socialism. He wished to differentiate between his scientific socialism and what he felt were the dreamy abstractions of others. The opposing faction was thus labeled by Marx as "utopian." To a large extent, Buber adds, this fight between the Marxists and the non-Marxists has conditioned our understanding of the word today.[3]

---

[1]Henrik F. Infield, *Utopia and Experiment* (New York: Frederick A. Praeger, 1955), pp. 9-10.

[2]Martin Buber, *Paths in Utopia* (translated by R.F.C. Hull), (London: Routledge and Kegan Paul, 1949), p. 5ff.

[3]Ibid., pp. 5f.

It is of course quite true that utopian writers have sometimes constructed impractical and purely escapist fantasies, just as serious writers on contemporary social problems have also presented us with impractical solutions to current problems. But to brand either group, *en masse,* as "impractical," "fantastic," or "escapist," just because some are, is a serious error; for many of those who have developed and pursued imaginery worlds, thus setting up a new myth or alternative by which man may judge the existing society, have often been guided by the most noble, rational, and constructive reasons.

It is important to note also that various utopian writers themselves have given different interpretations to the meaning of utopia. For Edward Bellamy, a utopian world, such as he envisioned, is not only desirable, but entirely practical. Many of the ideas which Bellamy advocated in 1888, and which were accordingly labeled as utopian, have since come into being as an integral part of our twentieth-century society. For Robert Owen, utopia is simply man's highest ideals, ideals which every man should have, or be striving for. He felt that man placed in a utopian setting is in a situation similar to that of a seedling which, when placed within the most advantageous soil and climatic conditions, achieves maximum growth and fructuousness. For William Morris, a utopian society meant not an extension of nineteenth or twentieth-century culture, but rather, a return to the past. It is not the thirtieth or the fortieth century that Morris extols, but rather the thirteenth-century and a return to the life lived by the craftsman. It is H. G. Wells, and not Morris, who looks eagerly forward to the advancement of society with all of its machines and technology. For Wells, utopia meant an unending search for progress. After one utopia was obtained, we would begin on another. It was this blind belief in progress which so disillusioned Wells later in life, as he saw man progressing not to a higher state, but from one great war to another. In Thomas Campanella's sense of utopia, we find an outline, neither for the past of Morris, nor for the distant future of Wells, but for immediate use. Campanella designed his utopia to be put into operation just as soon as the right party came into power at Naples. For Plato, the thought of utopia becomes a brilliant intellectual exercise, and in the hands of Samuel Butler and Aldous Huxley, it becomes a foil with which to prick at the inadequacies and the illogicalities of human societies. Thus, we see that there is no one all-encompassing meaning which fits utopia. It has as many shades of meaning as there are utopian writers.

Lewis Mumford divides all utopian works into two main classifications: "utopias of escape" and "utopias of reconstruction."[4] By the former, he means those works which create an ideal world not to be found on this earth. Such works may influence man to change his life or institutions in order to find this better world, but the aim is to reach a world apart from the one in which we live. An example of this would be Augustine's *City of God* which he contrasts with the "city of the world." The former is concerned with transcending this world, while the latter is concerned with man's material existence. Utopias of reconstruction, however, provide man with an insight as to what he might do to make his world better, or his life a little more meaningful. Although these utopias also may preach about some future life, the point of attack is always on the here and now.

None of the utopias included in this collection may be considered as escapist utopias. Even such a thinker as Andreae, who purportedly founded an ideal isle where Christians were not persecuted (because they were being persecuted in Europe) designed his ideas for application to the worldly scene, whenever and wherever tolerance permitted.

One further subclassification of utopias must be made, and that is between utopias which are speculative and those which are satirical. An example of a speculative utopia would be More's *Utopia* or Gott's *Nova Solyma*. Both of these men are proposing a future world which could conceivably exist, or come into being. There are no logical difficulties to their development.

Some good examples of satirical utopias would be Butler's *Erewhon* and Huxley's *Brave New World.* Although it is possible that such worlds as these could also come to pass, the purpose of their development was not to foreshadow future events, or even to wish for their coming, but rather, to point out, in some exaggerated way, deficiencies in the present mode of society. The utopian world which these men desired is described only indirectly, in terms of the evils which they would like to see eradicated.

One thing that I think we can say about all utopian works is that they have a meaning, or what might better be described as a message. The author, in each case, desires to put across to the reader some feeling, either intellectual or emotional, that he has. In the case of Huxley, it may be a cynical or pessimistic view about the future of society, whereas, in the case of Bellamy, he seems to be telling us

---

[4]Lewis Mumford, *The Story of Utopias* (New York: Boni and Liveright, 1922), p. 15ff.

what we may well expect to see in the future. Or, it can be, as in the case of Owen and Andreae, a statement of values and goals for man to follow in order to pursue a purer and more logical pattern of life.

Messages in utopias are not always clear. There has been a great deal of confusion, in many cases, about just what message an author intended to convey. All of the messages seem clear on the point, however, that there was something wrong, either in whole or in part, with the values which the author found within the society of which he was a member, and his utopian work stands as testimony of his effort to attack these values, and in most instances, to propose something better to take their place.

We also have to differentiate between what might be termed the "over-all" message and the meaning which individual portions of the work have for us. The over-all message of *Brave New World,* for example, seems to tell us what will happen if man continues to exercise his technological knowledge without an equal advancement in wisdom. In regard to education, however, one might adduce that he is telling us not only what might happen to man, but, through a renewed interest in educational conditioning, teaching machines, and an effort to imitate the formalized methods of the Russians, what *is* happening to man. The emphasis on conditioning, the development of organized class and social attitudes, which are portrayed so threateningly in *Brave New World,* are, in a sense, *fait accompli.* Likewise, in *Erewhon,* Butler seems to be going almost beyond the limits of reason to say that machines may someday develop a consciousness and control man, and yet, in a very real sense we could say that men today are slaves to the machines which they have invented.

In drawing up any utopian work, it would be quite useless for an author to produce any plan for a future society which is so far outside of our present values and symbols that we are unable to communicate with the author, or connect with his ideas in any real sense. When George Orwell wrote *1984,* he felt it necessary to append a glossary explaining the development and use of Newspeak. There is, then, an overlapping quality between the imaginary world which the author draws up and that within which the author lives, which cannot be escaped. Karl Mannheim[5] uses Landauer's terminology in this situation to distinguish between what he calls "topia" (the existing society) and "utopia" (the ideal society). In the former term, as Mannheim points out, we have a conception of

---

[5]Karl Mannheim, *Ideology and Utopia* (Translated by Louis Wirth and Edward Shils), (New York: Harcourt, Brace and Co., 1936), p. 193ff.

existence, and in the latter, a transcendence of existence. It is quite difficult, if not impossible, as Mannheim shows, to distinguish between topia and utopia in any absolute sense. They are not only overlapping, but are like the two opposite poles of a pendulum. Topias often evolve into utopias, which in turn become topias, and the process is an ever endless one in the social fabric of topias and utopias.

One of the great beliefs, however, of those who hold to a topian viewpoint is that the authors who conceive utopias are often unmindful of the practical problems of everyday life. I believe that a review of even such a limited amount of utopian writing as presented in this anthology will serve to show the falsity of this belief. Most, if not all, of the problems which were the concern of utopian writers have been great and important ones. The difference between topian and utopian writers has not been one, largely, of a difference in problems, but rather, a difference in approach to those problems. Whereas topian writers feel themselves able to deal with such problems within the existing framework of the society in which they live, utopians generally have no such belief. Indeed, it is the belief that they cannot cope in any real sense with the problems within the existing framework of contemporary society which makes them utopians. Their approach is to get outside of the general bounds of the cultural and social contemporary value system in order to look at problems afresh, without individual or social restraint.

It is quite true that the solutions to social problems which are offered by the utopianists frequently seem meaningless when applied to our present system. This is because, in the main, we cannot expect something taken out of one social context to fit neatly into another. What the utopians have pointed out, and understood better than anyone else, is that many of the great social problems of a society cannot be solved without changing the entire structure of the society within which these problems reside. It is the belief of many utopians that some of the things which we consider evils are really a part of the very institutions to which we swear allegiance, and that, there-fore, we cannot hope to eradicate these evils without a corres-ponding change in those same institutions. This is one of the principal reasons why the utopians have, by and large, placed such a high priority upon education. They saw a twofold necessity for education, first, for the purpose of educating man to the need for great and important changes, and secondly, they saw education as a vehicle for enabling man to adjust to these changes.

I think that we could say that most utopian writers not only have a high regard for education but are educationists themselves. We find, for example, that More advocated universal and compulsory education in the sixteenth century — an aim we are still trying to realize today. In the writings of Butler, also, we find many passages which clearly anticipate Dewey and the Progressive movement in education. Owen, as an educationist, is given credit as the founder of the first Infant School, and Skinner is well known for his work with teaching machines.

There is, to be sure, a great variation in the kinds of education proposed by utopians, both in form and content. In some utopias, such as *News from Nowhere,* we find that education is extremely permissive, and fishing and dancing are considered more important to learn than art and mathematics. In others, such as the *City of the Sun,* the most technical and scientific subjects are pursued as a means to the better life.

The method of teaching in most of our utopias also comes under close scrutiny. In some works, such as *A New View of Society* and the *Republic,* teachers are carefully selected, and carefully trained. In some others, boys untutored in all save living in a natural state become the tutors of the other children. The point of teacher training, in all cases, seems to depend importantly upon the type of educational philosophy or purpose of education proposed by the educational utopianist.

Although there are many political overtones in our utopian works, noticeable in Campanella's *City of the Sun,* and economic overtones, noticeable in Bellamy's *Looking Backward,* education becomes in both instances the main instrument for achieving the goals which the author had in mind. It is for this reason that many utopian writers have been accused of using education not as an end in itself but in order to achieve other desired goals. To a certain degree, this is true, but this is by no means universal among utopian writers. We must remember, however, that most of our utopians had a great desire to remake man and society, and found that their most effective instrument for achieving these purposes was education. Thus, they have often used education to proselytize for conservatism, liberalism, and religion, as well as irreligion, aristocracy, socialism, and communism, just as education is used to proselytize for these things today. Nor are all utopian writers free from the social biases and discriminations of which other writers are also susceptible. Wells was one who believed that some races were biologically superior to others, and also thought that man should try to develop a superrace of humans through a eugenic approach to living. Plato and More both incorporated slaves in their utopian plans, and Plato believed that there should be privileged classes in society, without the right of every man to participate in the development of the government. In stating these beliefs, the point is being made that our utopian writers, though often endowed with a penetrating and often supravisionary view of the future, as well as a comprehensive knowledge of history, were still subject to all of the intellectual ills which can beset men.

Utopians were limited, moreover, especially in the case of the earlier utopians, by a lack of understanding about science, as well as the inavailability of printed matter. Even modern utopians have been hampered by the often limited view of the society in which they were a part, as well as by the social, economic, and political pressures which existed at the time of their writing. The most important point about their writings, however, is that they expressed a new approach to problems and also gave new answers to some very old and troublesome social dilemmas. Nor does the value of the utopian spirit lie merely in its pragmatic usefulness. Utopians are responsible not only for giving us answers but also for raising many new, important, and significant questions, which we may use to increase our understanding of the social, political, and economic forces which surround us today, as well as those forces which influence and affect education.

In the selections which are being presented in this anthology, only a representative sample of utopian thought as it applies to education in Western civilization is being presented. After surveying all of the various writings on utopia written or translated in the English language, I have selected portions of some of those which deal specifically with this subject of education. Some well-known utopias, such as Bacon's unfinished *New Atlantis,* have not been included in this collection because they do not deal in any specific fashion with education, whereas some lesser known works which do, have been included.

The selections included in this work, which begin with Plato and end with Skinner, are placed in their chronological position, so that the reader may acquire a continous view of how the mind of each author operated during the period in which he was writing, as well as to show, in some cases, how an earlier work influenced the writing of a later one.

A critical introduction prefaces each selection in order to make certain historical and social facts clearer to the reader, and each selection is also preceded by a brief commentary which sets the selection in its proper context as a part of a total piece of writing. A brief biographical sketch of each author, as well as chapter bib-liographies, may be found at the end of the manuscript.

The majority of these selections on educational utopias have been presented in their entirety, which is to say that they comprise all that the author had to say about education in a particular work. Other pieces, either due to length or repetition of thought, have been presented in a synthesized fashion. A guiding rule in all cases, however, has been to present the author's basic educational concepts, or what might be termed his "philosophy of education." Thus, if the author had a definite Christian *Weltanschauung,* such as in the case of Andreae, the selection of passages made that fact clear to the reader, whereas, if the author was presenting a socialistic or a communistic point of view in regard to education, as in the case of Bellamy and Morris, respectively, that too was made clear to the reader. An effort was also made to capture the flavor of the original writings. Archaic langauge, when it did not distort the text, was kept in its original form, and only in a few rare instances was archaic spelling modernized.

In selecting the passages to be included in this book, which would be representative of a particular author's views on education, the problem was simplified when the author wrote only one book, and when the educational ideas contained in that work were located *en bloc.* The problem of selection increased proportionally, as in the case of Wells, when an author wrote a number of utopian works, many of which dealt with education, and therefore the selection of passages to be used had to remain my choice based upon a study of all of the author's writings about education in utopia. As the reader may readily understand, it is difficult if not impossible to separate in any complete way a writer's ideas about education in utopia from his ideas on other subjects, and it is also true that there is as yet no definitive analysis of any of the ideas expressed by the utopian writers included in this volume. Hopefully, the reader will read the entire text of the books suggested and "discover for himself" many of the new and exciting ideas about education that these writers have to offer.

This work was planned with the idea of clarifying the concept and role of utopia in educational thought, as well as to provide important source material and criticism for educators to use in planning practices and goals in education. This project not only points out how utopian thought has influenced education in the past but also points to the constructive influence that utopian ideas can have on education in the future.

INTRODUCTION

At this particular period in history, when man seems engaged in a frenetic search for new national goals, and correspondingly, new educational goals, we would do well to turn again to some of our utopian writers in order to benefit from their thinking upon this subject. There have been thinkers in all ages who have told us that we needed new purposes and new technological and social improvements, but very few of these critics have stated specifically what form these new improvements should take. Our utopians, however, have dared to accept this challenge. They not only say, for example, that education needs to be made better, but they show us what it is like, from their point of view, when it is made better.

Chapter One

PLATO AND THE *REPUBLIC*

It is very difficult to speak about Plato's ideas on education without discussing his philosophy as a whole, for his educational ideas are intelligible only when viewed as part of a larger design.

Plato believed that the world which we experience every day through our senses is not the real world, but merely a copy of it. The real world, he believed, is the world of Ideas. These Ideas have always existed in a state of perfectedness, and hence are not influenced by the things which happen in our world. The highest of these Ideas, he believed, was the Idea of the Good, toward which man should always be striving. There was to be no hope, however, of actually reaching this goal. But even to venture in the direction of the Good was commendable from Plato's point of view.

In the *Timaeus,* Plato tells us that it was the Demiurge who created these perfect ideas and also brought the copy world into being. The Demiurge created only one perfect Idea of a thing, but created thousands of copies of each thing in the world. For example, there is only one perfect man, according to Plato, but there are millions of men in the universe, each an imperfect copy of this ideal man.

Plato believed that man could come to know the real world, and contemplate true ideas, but only after the most vigorous kind of inquiry. Man's reason, he held, is hindered by the various aspects of the copy world of which he is a part; hence man must somehow transcend this world in order to contemplate real as opposed to "copy" truth.

This effort to transcend "copy" ideas invokes the fullest employment of man's reasoning powers. The person who uses his reasoning powers to their fullest extent embodies what Plato would term "the philosophic spirit." In the *Republic,* this idea is expressed in the Allegory of the Cave. In this highly instructive myth, the vast majority of mankind are pictured as living in a sort of subterranean cavern. From childhood, they have been chained so that they cannot move. All they can experience is a world of shadows projected by a

fire upon the far wall of a cave. Since this is the only world they have
ever known, they are convinced that this world of shadows is the
"real" world. Plato then asks us to imagine one of these beings set
free, able to stand up, turn his head, and walk out of the cave into
the sunlight. He would be dazzled at first but would gradually come
to realize that the shadows he had been seeing in the cave were
merely illusions, and that now he was getting a truer view of life. So
too, Plato believes that our lives are similar to those of the persons
who were chained inside the cave. We are accepting illusion, the
"copy" world, as the real world, and we have not yet attempted to
remove, by reflection, the chains of ignorance which bind us, so that
we too can move into the light of truth. Once we did, we would
begin to see our illusions for what they really are.

Plato further believed that the person who left the world of
shadows and penetrated into the world of light, or Ideas, had an
obligation to return to the cave (the world of false impressions) in
order to help and encourage others to leave the world of shadows
and seek the light of truth. He says that such a man would not want
to return again to the cave, and that the prisoners would not think
highly of his ideas, but that the philosophic man would realize it was
his duty to do so.

Plato believed that the surest instrument for transcending the
life of the Cave was reason, and further, that reason was on its
firmest footing when it used dialectical argument as its instrument.
The dialectical method, which consists of critical conversation, was
used by philosophers before Plato's time, but in Plato it reached its
highest point. Plato criticized the use of the dialectic when it was
developed merely for the sake of encouraging controversy. He
believed that it could become a pure intellectual discipline in itself,
and thus we see that in the *Republic,* education in the dialectic is
reserved only for those whose previous education has included the
most strenuous training in music, gymnastics, and mathematics.

The idea of harmony, which music, gymnastics, and mathematics supplies, is one of the central notions of Plato's philosophy.
He felt that all youths should be trained in these subjects until their
twentieth year. This period is designed to give the young man or
woman a feeling for harmony. After they have learned harmony as
mostly an instinctive feeling, a study of mathematics will reveal to
them the basic principles which underlie it. The principles of
harmony, established by the Demiurge, Plato believed, lie beneath
everything in the universe, and it is only mathematics, especially
geometry, which can cause us to turn our eyes away from the

fleeting and transitory world of sensation in which we live, so that we may contemplate ideal forms and ideal designs.

This feeling for harmony, as well as for symmetry and order, was expressed not only in Plato's philosophy, but in the attitude of the Greeks in general. It can be seen in their painting, sculpture, and architecture. A mathematical conception of harmony is, to a large extent, captured in the teachings of Pythagoras. It was Pythagoras who believed that the relationship between body and soul, a much-sought-after combination in art, could be found in harmony. Man, as well as society, he believed, was a harmony of opposites and discords, which could be explained mathematically.

In Plato's conception of utopia, the *Republic,* there is to be a harmonious balance of classes, consisting of the rulers, the guards, and the workers. Each person is to be placed in the category that best accords with his own capabilities. Through such an efficient system, Plato believes, each individual will contribute to society his own special aptitudes. The criterion for deciding to what group a person belonged was to be largely his or her performance in the educational processes of the state.

All persons, at least in the two higher classes of Plato's society, were to be given a general education, consisting of literature, music, and elementary mathematics, until they reached eighteen years of age. At this time, those who showed little ability for further training became part of the mercantile or working class. The others were given an additional two years of training in mathematics and warfare in order to become the guards of the state. A few others, who, during this time, had been noted for exceptional intellectual ability, were to be given an advanced course in mathematics in order to grasp the connections between the several branches of mathematics and their relationship to reality. After a further selection, with those who fail becoming part of the class of guards, the remainder, now aged between thirty and thirty-five, are to be given extensive training in the use of the dialectic, with particular emphasis on its serving to enlighten a student on the principles of morality. From thirty to thirty-five years of age, they are to serve in minor government posts, and at fifty years of age, the best remaining will become the rulers of the state, during which time they will divide their time between the practical duties of ruling and the philosophical duties of contemplation.

It is with the education of the rulers that Plato is most concerned, for these men are to become not only the leaders of a society but philosophers as well, men who will spend their lives in contemplation of the perfect Idea of the Good. The idea of the dialectic as the instrument for this aim is not considered in a person's early education, for Plato insists in at least a ten years' training period in mathematics before students are eligible for this subject. The teachers are to be true dialecticians. They will introduce perplexity where a conceited sense of knowledge existed before. By the use of appropriate questions the dialecticians will make the student aware of his ignorance, and then, jointly, they will attempt to clear the mind of false notions, so that a beginning may be made on the ascent toward the truth. Plato gives us a good example of this technique in the *Meno*. In this dialogue, it is discovered through skillful questioning that a slave boy, belonging to an Athenian named Meno, possesses some true knowledge, namely, "that the double of any square surface is the square of its diagonal." The slave knows this is so, but without realizing how he arrived at it, which brings us to the very important view of education that Plato held, *viz.,* that all knowledge was simply a matter of recollection. Plato believed that the Demiurge imparted a soul to each of us which contains true knowledge, but that this knowledge has been corrupted by being imprisoned in the body.

> *Ignorance as "bondage" and imprisonment of the mind is a theme of the* Phaedo. *In that dialogue the familiar Orphic myth is taken as illustrative of the human plight. Ignorance is the "entombment" of the soul in the body. Hence Socrates declares that the philosopher is one who seeks release from the body's "foolishness." He understands this liberation to be a deliverance from the "slough of ignorance" in which the human mind is sunk.*[1]

Plato does not fully accept the Doctrine of Reminiscence as outlined by Socrates, but there is a distinct relationship to this idea in the work of the dialectic, which is one of "arousement, purification, and quickening. It aims at recovering and renewing what is man's own. It is a refining process, as we are reminded in the Phaedo and again in the Sophist."[2]

Plato believed that men did not willingly err and accept false opinion, since this was contrary to the preference of the soul. We are reminded again of the Allegory of the Cave, where man finds himself unable to see the truth due to the chains which bind him. In order to see the truth, therefore, we must ascend from the cave by means of the dialectic, into the light of truth. Plato felt that we are often deceived by the appetitive faculties of the body into thinking that

[1] Robert E. Cushman, *Therapeia* (Chapel Hill: The University of North Carolina Press, 1958), p. 60.
[2] *Ibid*, p. 96.

certain evil desires are good ones. He believed that the purpose of education was to rid us of such false notions and put us once again into harmony with the divine workings of nature.

A fundamental premise, also, in regard to this belief, is Plato's conviction that once man knows the good, he will do the good. Plato believed that when men know what is the good thing to do, then they will no longer be capable of doing evil.

It is proficiency in the dialectic, Plato believes, which will help man to find truth, and which will produce the highest type of man — the philosopher. Plato felt that this was the kind of man we should want as the ruler of our state, even though he, himself, will not think highly of the task and will only accept the position as a matter of duty. Plato firmly believed in the principle that the state grew out of the kind of character which the ruler or rulers had. The problem of creating the best state, therefore, was correspondingly the problem of creating the best individual, since to Plato's mind, the state was just the individual writ large. It is important to note, too, that he believed that such individuals could only come about through a state which committed itself fully to education. This explains why Plato has transformed his entire utopian state into a gigantic educational institution, which, he is convinced, can create these superior individuals who are capable of leading the people toward this Idea of the Good.

Plato's conception of political authority was largely aristocratic, which is to say, that the people were to be ruled by an elite class of philosopher-kings. His theory of state called for the distribution of wealth according to need, and the placing of individuals into an ordered class-structured society. Plato also believed not only in the good of the individual but also in the good of the group, and saw no conflict between these two. The philosopher-kings were to so order the state that each man would contribute to the good of society as a whole, while that society, in turn, would contribute to his good as an individual, participating in the functioning of the state.

In most of Plato's writings, Socrates is the great protagonist, the skilled user of the dialectic. It is difficult to say where Socrates' ideas leave off and Plato's begin, though we are primarily led to think of Plato as a recorder with regard to the *Republic*. It is Socrates who, in the dialogues of Plato, challenges his fellow Athenians to defend their ideas in debate, and then, by transcending their ideas, creates great philosophical structures. Socrates is a seeker after truth, and yet he does not hesitate to use sophistry and irony when they serve to dispose men's minds to knowledge, as in the *Republic* when he states that the best guardian of money is the ablest thief.

The *Republic* has been considered by many to be the best of the dialogues. It is most certainly a great utopian work and one which is both practical and progressive. Its influence upon educators has been unparalleled in the history of thought.

REPUBLIC – Plato*

Socrates, who was Plato's teacher and who is considered to be one of the greatest of all philosophers, began, in a discussion at the house of Cephalus, a retired merchant living at Piraeus, to talk about the meaning of justice. This led to a consideration of ideal justice, and to the consideration of an ideal state. In a dialogue with Glaucon, a Sophist, Socrates discusses the course of education to be followed in this utopian state, to be known as the Republic, and in the following selection, begins to relate how the various studies are to be allotted.

It only remains, then, to draw up a scheme showing how, and to whom, these studies are to be allotted.

Clearly.

You remember what sort of people we chose earlier to be Rulers?

Of course I do.

In most respects, then, natures of that quality are to be selected: we shall prefer the steadiest, the bravest, and, so far as possible, the handsomest persons. But, besides that, we must look not only for generous and virile characters, but for gifts fitting them for this sort of education. They must be eager students and learn with ease, because the mind is more apt to shrink from severe study than from hard physical exercise, in which part of the burden falls upon the body. Also we must demand a good memory and a dogged appetite for hard work of every kind. How else can you expect a man to undergo all the hardships of bodily training and, on the top of that, to carry through such a long course of study?

He will certainly need every natural advantage.

At any rate, this explains what is wrong now with the position of Philosophy and why she has fallen into disrepute: as I said before, she ought never to have been wooed by the base-born, who are unworthy of her favors. To begin with, the genuine aspirant should not be one-sided in his love of work, liking one half of it and neglecting the other; as happens with one who throws himself into athletics and hunting and all sorts of bodily exertion, but hates the

*Plato, *Republic,* trans. Francis MacDonald Cornford (New York: Oxford University Press, 1945), Chapter 28, pp. 256-263. This work is believed to have been originally published in the first quarter of the fourth century B.C.

*trouble of learning anything from others or of thinking for himself.
His industry goes halting on one foot; and so it does too if it takes
the opposite direction.*

Quite true.

*Also with regard to truth, we shall count as equally crippled a
mind which, while it hates deliberate falsehood, cannot bear to tell
lies, and is very angry when others do so, yet complacently tolerates
involuntary error and is in no way vexed at being caught wallowing
in swinish ignorance. We must be no less on the watch to distinguish
the base metal from the true in respect of temperance, courage,
highmindedness, and every kind of virtue. A state which chooses its
rulers, or a man who chooses his friends, without a searching eye for
these qualities will find themselves, in respect of one or another of
them, cheated by a counterfeit or leaning on a broken reed. So all
such precautions are very much our concern. If we can find, for this
long course of training and study, men who are at all points sound of
limb and sound in mind, then Justice herself will have no fault to
find with us and we shall ensure the safety of our commonwealth
and its institutions. We should only ruin it by choosing pupils of a
different stamp; and moreover we should bring down upon philosophy an even greater storm of ridicule.*

That would be a discreditable result.

*It would. But at the moment I seem to be inviting ridicule
myself.*

In what way?

*By speaking with so much warmth and forgetting that these
speculations are only an amusement for our leisure. As I spoke, I
seemed to see Philosophy suffering undeserved insults, and was so
vexed with her persecutors that I lost my temper and became too
vehement.*

I did not think so as I listened.

*No, but I felt it myself. However, here is something we must
not forget. When we spoke earlier of selecting Rulers, we said we
should choose old men; but that will not do for the selection we are
making now. We must not let Solon persuade us that a man can learn
many things as he grows old; he could sooner learn to run. Youth is
the time for hard work of all sorts.*

Undoubtedly.

*Arthmetic, then, and geometry and all branches of the pre-
liminary education which is to pave the way for Dialectic should be
introduced in childhood; but not in the guise of compulsory
instruction, because for the free man there should be no element of
slavery in learning. Enforced exercise does no harm to the body, but*

enforced learning will not stay in the mind. So avoid compulsion, and let your children's lessons take the form of play. This will also help you to see what they are naturally fitted for.

That is a reasonable plan.

You remember, too, our children were to be taken to the wars on horseback to watch the fighting, and, when it was safe, brought close up like young hounds to be given a taste of blood.

I remember.

Then we must make a select list including everyone who shows forwardness in all these studies and exercises and dangers.

At what age?

As soon as they are released from the necessary physical training. This may take two or three years, during which nothing else can be done; for weariness and sleep are unfavorable to study. And at the same time, these exercises will provide not the least important test of character.

No doubt.

When that time is over, then, some of those who are now twenty years old will be selected for higher privileges. The detached studies in which they were educated as children will now be brought together in a comprehensive view of their connections with one another and with reality.

Certainly that is the only kind of knowledge which takes firm root in the mind.

Yes, and the chief test of a natural gift for Dialectic, which is the same thing as the ability to see the connections of things.

I agree.

You will keep an eye, then, on these qualities and make a further selection of those who possess them in the highest degree and show most steadfastness in study as well as in warfare and in their other duties. When they reach thirty they will be promoted to still higher privileges and tested by the power of Dialectic, to see which can dispense with sight and the other senses and follow truth into the region of pure reality. And here, my friend, you will need the greatest watchfulness.

Why in particular?

You must have seen how much harm is done now by philosophical discussion — how it infects people with a spirit of lawlessness.

Yes, I have.

Does that surprise you? Can you not make allowances for them? Imagine a child brought up in a rich family with powerful connections and surrounded by a host of flatterers; and suppose that, when he comes to manhood, he learns that he is not the son of those who call themselves his parents and his true father and mother are not to be found. Can you guess how he would feel towards his supposed parents and towards his flatterers before he knew about his parentage and after learning the truth? Or shall I tell you what I should expect?

Please do.

I should say that, so long as he did not know the truth, he would have more respect for his reputed parents and family than for the flatterers, and be less inclined to neglect them in distress or to be insubordinate in word or deed; and in important matters the flatterers would have less influence with him. But when he learnt the facts, his respect would be transferred to them; their influence would increase, and he would openly associate with them and adopt their standards of behavior, paying no heed to his reputed father and family, unless his disposition were remarkably good.

Yes, all that would be likely to happen. But how does your illustration apply to people who are beginning to take part in philosophical discussions?

In this way. There are certain beliefs about right and honorable conduct, which we have been brought up from childhood to regard with the same sort of reverent obedience that is shown to parents. In opposition to these, other courses attract us with flattering promises of pleasure; though a moderately good character will resist such blandishments and remain loyal to the beliefs of his fathers. But now suppose him confronted by the question, What does 'honorable' mean? He gives the answer he has been taught by the lawgiver, but he is argued out of his position. He is refuted again and again from many different points of view and at last reduced to thinking that what he called honorable might just as well be called disgraceful. He comes to the same conclusion about justice, goodness, and all the things he most revered. What will become now of his old respect and obedience?

Obviously they cannot continue as before.

And when he has disowned these discredited principles and failed to find the true ones, naturally he can only turn to the life which flatters his desires; and we shall see him renounce all morality and become a lawless rebel. If this is the natural consequence of plunging the young into philosophical discussion, ought we not to make allowances, as I said before?

Yes, and be sorry for them too.

Then, if you do not want to be sorry for those pupils of yours who have reached the age of thirty, you must be very careful how

you introduce them to such discussions. One great precaution is to
forbid their taking part while they are still young. You must have
seen how youngsters, when they get their first taste of it, treat
argument as a form of sport solely for purposes of contradiction.
When someone has proved them wrong, they copy his methods to
confute others, delighting like puppies in tugging and tearing at
anyone who comes near them. And so, after a long course of proving
others wrong and being proved wrong themselves, they rush to the
conclusion that all they once believed is false; and the result is that in
the eyes of the world they discredit, not themselves only, but the
whole business of philosphy. An older man will not share this craze
for making a sport of contradiction. He will prefer to take for his
model the conversation of one who is bent on seeking truth, and his
own reasonableness will bring credit on the pursuit. We meant to
ensure this result by all that we said earlier against the present
practice of admitting anybody, however unfit, to philosophic discussions, and about the need for disciplined and steadfast
character.

Certainly.

If a man, then, is to devote himself to such discussion as
continuously and exclusively as he gave himself up earlier to the
corresponding training of his body, will twice as long a time be
enough?

Do you mean six years or four?

No matter; let us say five. For after that they must be sent
down again into that Cave we spoke of and compelled to take
military commands and other offices suitable to the young, so that
they may not be behind their fellow citizens in experience. And at
this stage they must once more be tested to see whether they will
stand firm against all seductions.

How much time do you allow for this?

Fifteen years. Then, when they are fifty, those who have come
safely through and proved the best at all points in action and in
study must be brought at last to the goal. They must lift up the eye
of the soul to gaze on that which sheds light on all things; and when
they have seen the Good itself, take it as a pattern for the right
ordering of the state and of the individual, themselves included. For
the rest of their lives, most of their time will be spent in study; but
they will all take their turn at the troublesome duties of public life
and act as Rulers for their country's sake, not regarding it as a
distinction, but as an unavoidable task. And so, when each generation has educated others like themselves to take their place as
Guardians of the commonwealth, they will depart to dwell in the
Islands of the Blest. The state will set up monuments for them and

sacrifices, honoring them as divinities, if the Pythian Oracle approves, or at least as men blest with a godlike spirit.

That is a fine portrait of our Rulers, Socrates.

Yes, Glaucon, and you must not forget that some of them will be women. All I have been saying applies just as much to any women who are found to have the necessary gifts.

Quite right, if they are to share equally with the men in everything, as we said.

Well then, said I, do you agree that our scheme of a commonwealth and its constitution has not been a mere daydream? Difficult it may be, but possible, though only on the one condition we laid down, that genuine philosophers — one or more of them — shall come into power in a state; men who will despise all existing honors as mean and worthless, caring only for the right and the honors to be gained from that, and above all for justice as the one indispensable thing in whose service and maintenance they will reorganize their own state.

How will they do that?

They must send out into the country all citizens who are above ten years old, take over the children, away from the present habits and manners of their parents, and bring them up in their own ways under the institutions we have described. Would not that be the quickest and easiest way in which our polity could be established, so as to prosper and be a blessing to any nation in which it might arise?

Yes, certainly; and I think, Socrates, you have satisfactorily explained how, if ever, it might come into being.

Have we now said enough, then, about this commonwealth and also about the corresponding type of man; for it must be clear what sort of person we shall expect him to be?

It is clear; and to answer your question, I believe our account is complete.

Chapter Two

THOMAS MORE AND UTOPIA

More's *Utopia* is considered by many to be the greatest of all utopian works. It was More who coined the word "Utopia," under which similar works dealing with imaginary social orders have been categorized.

The writing of *Utopia*, or at least the idea for it, is believed to have been conceived during a six month's residence in Flanders where More was engaged in official duties for the government of England. It was in Antwerp that More met Peter Giles, a mutual friend of Erasmus, who, in the story of *Utopia*, introduces More to the sailor-philosopher Raphael Hythloday.

In writing *Utopia*, More drew upon his association with Giles and Erasmus, as well as the writings of the Greeks and the travel reports of great explorers, such as Vespucci. More composed this work at a time prior to the Protestant Reformation, and some of the great social ideas and social ferment which were developing during the time can be found in its pages. *Utopia* also serves to express some of the concern which was felt in sixteenth-century intellectual circles about the importance of a study of Greek. More was himself a classical scholar, proficient in the study of Greek and Latin, as were most scholars at that time. The classical Greek and Latin writings were believed to be only truly fruitful when read in their original state. This explains why More, who has been called a "most typical Englishman of his day," wrote *Utopia* in Latin, which was not translated into English until some thirty-five years later.

More was a great admirer of the Greeks. He felt that a knowledge of Greek should be a prerequisite to any classical or philosophical study, and he uses Greek allusions frequently in his writing: the work "Utopia," for example, comes from the Greek, meaning "no place"; Amaurote, the capital of Utopia, means "the phantom city"; and its great river Anyder, "the waterless river." There are many such paradoxical expressions taken from the Greek language throughout the Latin edition of the manuscript.

Of all the Greeks, More was especially fond of Plato. In many ways, Plato's *Republic* can be considered as the prototype of *Utopia.* One critic called More's *Utopia* a "Christian version of Plato's *Republic,* adapted to the new social order."[1]

Both Plato and More propose a communistic plan for a future society, the distinction being that in More's case it is Christian communism. More was greatly disturbed by the social ills of his day, especially by the English leaders of his day, and he seems to find an ally in Plato, who experienced similar feelings with regard to Hellenic society. Throughout *Utopia* More makes constant reference to the *Republic* which was decidedly influential in the writing of his work. Dudok[2] points out that the *Republic* and *Utopia* are not only similar in ideas but also in structure, since both of these works can be divided into two distinct parts. In More's case, the division is easily discernable. Book I contains a diatribe on the social ills of England, whereas Book II is concerned with a description of the island of Utopia. According to Dudok, the *Republic* can be divided into two parts also, the first part being Books I to III, which contains the description of a state formed in accordance with Hellenic notions, and then in Books V to X where Plato transforms the Hellenic State into an ideal City. Both cities, the Hellenic and the Utopian one, are also similar in that they are both philosophic cities, and the people are also given the kind of education which a philosophic perspective would advise. Dudok also draws a comparison between Hythloday and Socrates.

> *Both move in an atmosphere of irony, both are now jesting, now in earnest, now provoking, now appeasing, and each of the interrogators is puzzled to gather from the other's looks or tone whether he is speaking seriously, or whether he is merely joking. And again, they agree in the essential point, that although they will give reins to their humor, their purpose is primarily a serious one.[3]*

There are, however, as many fundamental differences between the two works as there are similarities. There is no division of people into classes in *Utopia* such as the division of people in the Republic into rulers, guardians, and workers. In *Utopia,* all men are equal, and there is no privileged class. It could even be said that More raises the lower classes to a more than equal status because of his great regard

[1]H. de B. Gibbins, *English Social Reformers* (London: Methuen and Co., 1892, p. 59.

[2]Gerald Dudok, *Sir Thomas More and His Utopia* (Amsterdam: H. J. Paris, 1924), pp. 72-73.

[3]*Ibid.,* p. 94.

for agriculture. In *Utopia*, agriculture is a matter of great concern, and everyone is required not only to know something about it, but to participate in it in actual practice for a minimum period of two years.

Plato had his soldiers, who were to be trained rigorously for warfaring, in order to protect the state. More has no soldiers in *Utopia*. He believed that people should be trained for peace, not war.

Some critics believe that the influence of Amerigo Vespucci has generally been ignored or underrated as a formative force in the writing of *Utopia*. Parks[4] believes that More took his travel ideas about the voyage of Hythloday to the mythical land of the Utopians from the *Lettera* of Vespucci which tell of his fourth voyage to Brazil in 1503-1504. According to Parks' calculations, the island of Utopia, as charted by More, would correspond roughly to the position of Tasmania.

In the second book of *Utopia*, Raphael Hythloday tells about the various customs and institutions which make up this new island he has discovered. There are, for example, fifty-four cities on the island of Utopia. These cities are no closer than twenty-four miles distance, and the legal jurisdiction of each city extends for twenty miles. There are many farmhouses outside of the towns, and each country family has no less than forty men and women in it. There is a master and a mistress set over each of these large families, and over every thirty families there is a magistrate, known as the Syphogrant. Over every ten Syphogrants there is a higher magistrate called the Tranibor. The Syphogrants, who number two-hundred, choose the great Prince of Utopia, who will rule over them all. This Prince is appointed for life, unless removed on the charge of attempting to enslave the people. The Tranibors consult with the Prince on every third day, in order to discuss the general and private affairs of the people.

In the towns, there are such trades as the manufacturing of wool and flax, masonry, smithing, and carpentry. All persons, whether in town or country, wear the same style of clothes, which cannot be bought but must be made by the members of the family themselves. More felt strongly about the importance of family ties, and he felt that living and working together in close harmony were conducive to the better instincts of man. It was the duty of the Syphogrants to see to it that each family member was employed in

---

[4] George B. Parks, "More's Utopia and Geography," *The Journal of English and Germanic Philology*, 37:224-236, April, 1938.

some useful enterprise, with adequate time allowed them for play and study.

More gives considerable attention to the education of the Utopians. Like Robert Owen, he greatly believed in the influence and importance of environmental factors and felt that the kind of education which children receive, due to the conditions and ideas to which they are exposed while young, is greatly responsible for the ideas and feelings which they hold as adults. His ideas on educational reform cannot be separated from other aspects of the new society, such as the legal code, and he felt that if the State was responsible, either directly or indirectly, for its citizens being ill educated, then that same State had no right to try those citizens for crimes committed because of lack of education, or because of the improper kind of education which they received. He strongly believed that the early formative education which a child receives should stress, above all, the futility of pursuing wealth and vain honors.

There are three general classes of students in *Utopia:* the scholars, the children of school age, and the rest of the people. More was a strong believer in universal education, and believed that all people should participate in the study of literature, and perhaps, also, the sciences. This is the prime reason for the shortness of working hours in Utopia, six hours a day, so that the people may be free to pursue the pleasures of the mind (Knowledge), as well as the pleasures of the body (exercise and play), which prepare the body for study. More also advocates early morning lectures, which the people can attend before they go to work. And work, too, is considered an educational experience in *Utopia.* It is for this reason that the entire populace is trained in childhood for agriculture, and why they must participate in it.

There is no formal kind of curriculum in Utopia, but the teachers who are in charge of the children are ever on the alert for those children who exhibit an extraordinary disposition for learning. Such children are then excused from a certain portion of manual labor, so that they can spend additional time exclusively in the cultivation of the mind.

More had very strong religious convictions, and these carried over into the writing of *Utopia.* He entrusts the education of youth to the church, which occupies a dominant role in this regard. The Utopians themselves, while not espousing any one particular kind of religion, are permeated with a kind of pantheism, and there are church services, known as "union services," where all sects can participate together in harmony.

Since More, unlike Plato, set his *Utopia* in actual and not mythical time, it can be looked upon as a more practical kind of society than the *Republic*. More is proposing a plan which he feels is workable. He does not try to deny man his pleasures, nor does he expect all of his citizens to become great men or women. He desires only that they enjoy a reasonable amount of happiness, and this, he feels, can be achieved through accepting a harmonious balance of work, study, and religion.

UTOPIA – Thomas More*

One morning while leaving the Cathedral Church in Antwerp, More meets Peter Giles, "a man of great honor," who introduces him to the Portuguese seaman and explorer Raphael Hythloday. The three of them then go to More's house where Hythloday tells them about his adventures, and the discovery of an island, "The Ideal Republic Which Is the New Island of Utopia." In the following passages, he tells of their manner of education.

AGRICULTURE is that which is so universally understood among them that no person, either man or woman, is ignorant of it; they are instructed in it from their childhood, partly by what they learn at school, and partly by practice; they being led out often into the fields, about the town, where they not only see others at work, but are likewise exercised in it themselves. Besides agriculture, which is so common to them all, every man has some peculiar trade to which he applies himself, such as the manufacture of wool, or flax, masonry, smith's work, or carpenter's work; for there is no sort of trade that is in great esteem among them. Throughout the island they wear the same sort of clothes without any other distinction except what is necessary to distinguish the two sexes, and the married and unmarried. The fashion never alters; and as it is neither disagreeable nor uneasy, so it is suited to the climate, and calculated both for their summers and winters. Every family makes their own clothes, but all among them, women as well as men, learn one or other of the trades formerly mentioned. Women, for the most part, deal in wool and flax, which suit best with their weakness, leaving the ruder trades to the men. The same trade generally passes down from father to son, inclinations often following descent; but if any man's genius lies another way, he is by adoption translated into a family that deals in the trade to which he is inclined; and when that is to be done, care is taken not only by his father, but by the magistrate, that he may be put to a discreet good man. And if after a person has learned one

*Thomas More, *Utopia* (in *Ideal Empires and Republics*. London: M. Walter Dunne, 1901), pp. 168-172, 183-186, 195-198. This work was originally published in Latin in 1516.

trade, he desires to learn another, that is also allowed, and is managed in the same manner as the former. When he has learned both, he follows that which he likes best, unless the public has more occasion for the other.

The chief and almost the only business of the Syphogrants is to take care that no man may live idle, but that every one may follow his trade diligently; yet they do not wear themselves out with perpetual toil from morning to night as if they were beasts of burden, which as it is indeed a heavy slavery, so it is everywhere the common course of life among all mechanics except the Utopians; but they, dividing the day and night into twenty-four hours, appoint six of these for work; three of which are before dinner; and three after. They then sup, and at eight o'clock, counting from noon, go to bed and sleep eight hours. The rest of their time besides that taken up in work, eating and sleeping, is left to every man's discretion; yet they are not to abuse that interval to luxury and idleness but must employ it in some proper exercise according to their various inclinations, which is for the most part reading. It is ordinary to have public lectures every morning before daybreak; at which none are obliged to appear but those who are marked out for literature; yet a great many, both men and women of all ranks, go to hear lectures of one sort or other, according to their inclinations. But if others, that are not made for contemplation, choose rather to employ themselves at that time in their trades, as many of them do, they are not hindered, but are rather commended, as men that take care to serve their country. After supper, they spend an hour in some diversion, in summer in their gardens, and in winter in the halls where they eat; where they entertain each other, either with music or discourse. They do not so much know dice or any such foolish and mischievous games; they have, however, two sorts of games not unlike our chess; the one is between several members, in which one number, as it were, consumes another; the other resembles a battle between the virtues and the vices, in which the enmity in the vices among themselves, and their agreement against virtue is not unpleasantly represented; together with the special oppositions between the particular virtues and vices; as also the methods by which vice either openly assaults or secretly undermines virtue; and virtue on the other hand resists it. But the time appointed for labor is to be narrowly examined, otherwise you may imagine, that since there are only six hours appointed for work, they may fall under a scarcity of necessary provisions. But it is so far from being true, that this time is not sufficient for supplying them with plenty of all things, either necessary or convenient; that it is rather too much; and this you will easily apprehend if you consider how great a part of all other nations is quite idle. First, women generally do little, who are the half of mankind; and if some few women are diligent, their husbands are idle; then consider the great company of idle priests, and of those that are called religious men; add to these all rich men, chiefly those that have estates in land, who are called noblemen and gentlemen, together with their families, made up of idle persons, that are kept more for show than use; add to these all those strong and lusty beggars that go about pretending some disease in excuse for their begging; and upon the whole account you will find that the number of those by whose labors mankind is supplied is much less than you perhaps imagined. Then consider how few of those that work are employed in labors that are of real service; for we who measure all things by money give rise to many trades that are both vain and superfluous and serve only to support riot and luxury. For if those who work were employed only in such things as the conveniences of life require, there would be such an abundance of them, and the prices of them would so sink, that tradesmen could not be maintained by their gains; if all those who labor about useless things were set to more profitable employment, and if all they that languish but their lives in sloth and idleness, every one of whom consumes as much as any two of the men that are at work, were forced to labor, you may easily imagine that a small proportion of time would serve for doing all that is either necessary, profitable, or pleasant to mankind, especially while pleasure is kept within its due bounds. This appears very plainly in Utopia, for there, in a great city, and in all the territory that lies round it, you can scarce find five hundred, either men or women, by their age and strength, are capable of labor, that are not engaged in it; even the Syphogrants, though excused by the law, yet do not excuse themselves, but work, that by their examples they may incite the industry of the rest of the people. The like exemption is allowed to those, who being recommended to the people by the priests, are by the secret suffrages of the Syphogrants privileged from labor, that they may apply themselves wholly to study; and if any of these fall short of those hopes that they seemed at first to give, they are obliged to return to work. And sometimes a mechanic that so employs his leisure hours as to make a considerable advancement in learning is eased from being a tradesman, and ranked among their learned men. Out of these they choose their ambassadors, their priests, their Tranibors, and the Prince himself; anciently called their Barzenes, but called of late their Ademus.

The Utopians wonder how any man should be so much taken with the glaring doubtful luster of a jewel or a stone that can look up to a star, or to the sun himself; or how any should value himself because his cloth is made of a finer thread: for how fine soever that thread may be, it was once no better than the fleece of a sheep, and that sheep was a sheep still for all its wearing it. They wonder much to hear that gold, which in itself is so useless a thing, should be everywhere so much esteemed, that even men for whom it was made, and by whom it has its value, should yet be thought of less value than this metal. That a man of lead, who has no more sense than a log of wood, and is as bad as he is foolish, should have many wise and good men to serve him only because he has a great heap of that metal; and that if it should happen that by some accident or trick of law (which sometimes produces as great changes as chance itself) all this wealth should pass from the master to the meanest varlet of his whole family, he himself would very soon become one of his servants, as if he were a thing that belonged to his wealth, and so were bound to follow its fortune. But they much more admire and detest the folly of those who when they see a rich man, though they neither owe him anything, nor are in any sort dependent on his bounty, yet merely because he is rich give him little less than divine honors; even though they know him to be so covetous and base-minded, that notwithstanding all his wealth, he will not part with one farthing of it to them as long as he lives.

These and such like notions have that people imbibed, partly from their education, being bred in a country whose customs and laws are opposite to all such foolish maxims, and partly from their learning and studies; for though there are but few in any town that are so wholly excused from labor as to give themselves entirely up to their studies, these being only such persons as discover from their childhood an extraordinary capacity and disposition for letters; yet their children, and a great part of the nation, both men and women, are taught to spend those hours in which they are not obliged to work in reading: and this they do through the whole progress of life. They have all their learning in their own tongue, which is both a copious and pleasant language, and in which a man can fully express his mind. It runs over a great tract of many countries, but it is not equally pure in all places. They had never so much as heard of the names of any of those philosophers that are so famous in these parts of the world before we went among them; and yet they had made the same discoveries as the Greeks, both in music, logic, arithmetic, and geometry. But as they are almost in everything equal to the ancient philosophers, so they far exceed our modern logicians; for

*they have never yet fallen upon the barbarous niceties that our youth
are forced to learn in those trifling logical schools that are among us;
they are so far from minding chimeras, and fantastical images made
in the mind, that none of them could comprehend what we meant
when we talked to them of a man in the abstract, as common to all
men in particular (so that though we spoke of him as a thing that we
could point at with our fingers, yet none of them could perceive
him), and yet distinct from every one, as if he were some monstrous
Colossus or giant. Yet for all this ignorance of these empty notions,
they know astronomy, and were perfectly acquainted with the
motions of the heavenly bodies, and have many instruments, well
contrived and divided, by which they very accurately compute the
course and positions of the sun, moon, and stars. But for the cheat of
divining the stars by their oppositions or conjunctions, it has not so
much as entered into their thoughts.They have a particular sagacity,
founded upon much observation, in judging of the weather, by which
they know when they may look for rain, wind, or other alterations in
the air; but as to the philosophy of these things, the causes of the
saltness of the sea, of its ebbing and flowing, and of the origin and
nature both of the heavens and the earth; they dispute of them,
partly as our ancient philosophers have done, and partly upon some
new hypothesis, in which, as they differ from them, so they do not
in all things agree among themselves.*

*As to moral philosophy, they have the same disputes among
them as we have here: they examine what are properly good both for
the body and the mind, and whether any outward thing can be called
truly good, or if that term belongs only to the endowments of the
soul. They inquire likewise into the nature of virtue and pleasure; but
their chief dispute is concerning the happiness of a man, and wherein
it consists? Whether in some one thing, or in a great many? They
seem, indeed, more inclinable to that opinion that places, if not the
whole, yet the chief part of a man's happiness in pleasure; and what
may seem more strange, they make use of arguments even from
religion, notwithstanding its severity and roughness, for the support
of that opinion so indulgent to pleasure; for they never dispute
concerning happiness without fetching some arguments from the
principles of religion, as well as from natural reason, since without
the former they reckon that all our inquiries after happiness must be
but conjectural and defective.*

   The people are industrious, apt to learn, as well as cheerful and pleasant; and none can endure more labor when it is necessary; but except in that case they love their ease. They are unwearied pursuers of knowledge; for when we had given them some hints of the learning and discipline of the Greeks, concerning whom we only instructed them (for we know that there was nothing among the Romans, except their historians and their poets, that they would value much), it was strange to see how eagerly they were set on learning that language. We began to read a little of it to them, rather in compliance with their importunity, than out of any hopes of their reaping from it any great advantage. But after a very short trial we found they made such progress that we saw our labor was like to be more successful than we could have expected. They learned to write their characters and to pronounce their language so exactly, had so quick an apprehension, they remembered it so faithfully, and became so ready and correct in the use of it, that it would have looked like a miracle if the greater part of those whom we taught had not been men both of extraordinary capacity and a fit age for instruction. They were for the greatest part chosen from among their learned men by their chief council, though some studied it of their own accord. In three years' time they became masters of the whole language, so that they read the best of the Greek authors very exactly. I am indeed apt to think that they learned that language the more easily from its having some relation to their own. I believe that they were a colony of the Greeks; for though their language comes nearer the Persian, yet they retain many names both for their towns and magistrates that are of Greek derivation. I happened to carry a great many books with me, instead of merchandise, when I sailed my fourth voyage; for I was so far from thinking of soon coming back that I rather thought never to have returned at all, and I gave them all my books, among which were many of Plato's and some of Aristotle's works. I had also Theophrastus on Plants, which to my great regret, was imperfect; for having laid it carelessly by, while we were at sea, a monkey seized upon it, and in many places tore out the leaves. They have no books of grammar but Lascares, for I did not carry Theodorus with me; nor have they any dictionaries but Hesichius and Dioscorides. They esteem Plutarch highly, and were much taken with Lucian's wit, and with his pleasant way of writing. As for the poets, they have Aristophanes, Homer, Euripides, and Sophocles of Aldus's edition; and for historians Thucydides, Herodotus and Herodian. One of my companions, Thricius Apinatus, happened to carry with him some of Hippocrates's works, and Galen's Microtechne, which they hold in great estimation; for though there is no nation in the world that needs physic so little as they do, yet there is not any that honors it so much: they reckon the knowledge of it one of the pleasantest and most profitable parts of philosophy, by which, as they search into the secrets of Nature, so they not only find this study highly agreeable, but think that such inquiries are very acceptable to the Author of Nature; and imagine that as he, like the inventors of curious engines among mankind, has exposed this great machine of the universe to the view of the only creatures capable of contemplating it, so an exact and curious observer who admires his workmanship is much more acceptable to him than one of the herd, who like a beast incapable of reason looks on this glorious scene with the eyes of a dull and unconcerned spectator.

The minds of the Utopians when fenced with a love for learning, are very ingenious in discovering all such arts as are necessary to carry it to perfection. Two things they owe to us, the manufacture of paper, and the art of printing: yet they are not so entirely indebted to us for these discoveries, but that a great part of the invention was their own. We showed them some books printed by Aldus, we explained to them the way of making paper, and the mystery of printing; but as we had never practiced these arts, we described them in a crude and superficial manner. They seized the hints we gave the.n, and though at first they could not arrive at perfection, yet by making many essays they at last found out and corrected all their errors and conquered every difficulty. Before this they only wrote on parchment, on reeds, or on the barks of trees; but now they have established the manufactures of paper, and set up printing presses, so that if they had but a good number of Greek authors they would be quickly supplied with many copies of them: at present, though they have no more than those I have mentioned, yet by several impressions they have multiplied them into many thousands. If any man were to go among them that had some extraordinary talent or that by much traveling had observed the customs of many nations (which made us to be so well received), he would receive a hearty welcome; for they are very desirous to know the state of the whole world.

Chapter Three

THOMAS CAMPANELLA
AND CITY OF THE SUN

Campanella's *City of the Sun* was written in the same year as Bacon's *New Atlantis.* Blodgett[1] points out that it is difficult to draw parallels between the two works, for where Campanella advocates communism, Bacon extols the family; and where Campanella describes a theocracy, Bacon describes a kingdom. However, she believes it entirely possible that Bacon read *City of the Sun* before or during the writing of *New Atlantis.*

Campanella was a man who was well versed in the arts and sciences of his day. Although he was never quite free of the medieval influence, he rejected Aristotelianism, which he considered a pagan philosophy, and accepted the scientific theories of Nicholas of Cusa and Telesio. He believed that philosophy should be based on experience, and verified by actual observation whenever possible. Like Augustine and Descartes, he believed in the certainty of individual consciousness, and his proof of God was the fact that our consciousness contains the idea of an Infinite Being. Our idea of the Infinite, he believed, could only come from some infinite source, *i.e.,* God. Campanella assigned a threefold content to this consciousness — knowledge, will, and love. He believed that the perfection of these three aspects of consciousness would lead us into communion with true religion and with God. He felt that the further removed from God we are, the more are these three aspects of consciousness imperfect, and the greater is our not-being, which is characterized by our ignorance, impotence, and hatred.

The influence of Plato can clearly be seen in *City of the Sun,* and Campanella readily acknowledges his debt to the Greeks. In the *City of the Sun,* just as in the *Republic,* there is a communism of goods and wives, and both states are to be ruled by philosophers. In Campanella's case, however, the distinction is that the rulers are philosopher-priests. It is the philosopher-priests who attempt to lead

---

[1]Eleanor Dickinson Blodgett, "Bacon's New Atlantis and Campanella's Civitas Solis: A Study in Relationships," *Publications of the Modern Language Association,* 46:763-780, September, 1931.

the people in accordance with God and to aid them in the increased perfection of knowledge, will, and love. Campanella, like Plato, had no fear that education unfitted man for practical and political authority. He felt that the educated man was the most qualified to run the state.

Although Campanella agreed with Machiavelli that the end justified the means and that the philosopher-priests had the right to command the populace to any action, however seemingly ignoble, which would aid their religious journey, yet he disagreed with the Machiavellian idea that religion was to be an instrument of government. For Campanella, it was just the other way around, and he maintained the superiority of the Church to the State and all temporal authority to the Pope.

While at a monastery in Stilo, Campanella wrote a political treatise which stated the belief of the author that Spain should create a theocratic universal republic. His dream was that there should be a universal republic, governed by the Pope and defended by the French or Spanish monarchy. He was accused of conspiring to overthrow the Kingdom of Naples and brought to trial. He was subsequently declared insane, which prevented his being condemned to death; but he was tortured and then imprisoned in the dungeons of various Neapolitan prisons for a total period of twenty-seven years. Campanella was not the only one to be condemned because of his writings. Giordano Bruno, a contemporary, was not only imprisoned but burned at the stake by the Inquisition in 1600.

Campanella had great difficulty in fitting together the ideas of Telesio and Galileo with the Thomistic, Augustinian, Platonic, and Neo-Platonic philosophies, which he also believed in. He defended Telesio from attack in his *Philosophia Sensibus demonstrata,* which was published in 1591, and he composed *The Defense of Galileo* in 1616. In both of these works he asks for freedom of investigation for Copernican astronomy. He believed that attacks on Telesio, Galileo, and Copernicus sprang from either a misunderstanding of the scriptures, a blind acceptance of pagan belief, or jealousy. In the introduction to *The Defense of Galileo,* Grant McColley says of Campanella:

> *In his individualism, his eclecticism and catholicity of mind, as well as in his desire to take all knowledge as his province, Campanella was a true son of the Renaissance. Included among and often fused with his own beliefs are a multitude of ideas and conceptions drawn from a wide variety of sources: the Christian mystics, the Fathers and Scholastics, especially Albertus Magnus and Saint Thomas, the Jewish and Arabian schools, Pythagoras, Plato, Aristotle, Zeno, Empedocles,*

Copernicus, Telsio, and Galileo. We doubtless should question the encomium of the learned Cardinal Pallavicini, who described Campanella as a "man who had read and who remembered all things" but we may accept, I believe, the statement of a second contemporary, Vincent Baron, that he was a philosopher of "extraordinary gifts, skilled in mathematics, astrology, medicine and other sciences."[2]

In *City of the Sun,* Campanella introduces his readers to a communistic society run by philosopher-priests, who have earned their offices through training and education. The supreme ruler is a priest called Metaphysic, who is assisted by three priest-princes: Power, Wisdom, and Love. All learning in *City of the Sun* is under the direction of the prince called Wisdom. He has thirteen assistants who are all doctors of learning, each representing one branch of education.

Since Campanella felt that most people educate their children badly, he declared that when children reach their third year, they must be committed into the care of the state. At this time, their formal education begins. They are not taught so much out of books, however, but audio-visually, *viz.,* by objects and drawings presented and explained to them.

Campanella believed, as did Plato, that the entire state should be a gigantic educational institution, with every person either a teacher or a pupil. In the *City of the Sun,* the seven walls which surround the city of the Solarians are painted with great drawings which aid in the education of all the citizens. There are mathematical figures, drawings of the earth, paintings of metals, medicines, *etc.* Campanella believed that through such a technique, the essential things in life would be learned "without toil and as if for pleasure."

The Solarians also held work to be an enobling and a very necessary part of education. The children, both boys and girls, were to be taught such practical things as shoemaking, cooking, and carpentry. The child thus engages in mental and manual exercises from three to seven, after which time it is the special function of the teachers to discern the special aptitudes of each pupil. When the child's specialty has been discovered, he is given further training in this area. The purpose of this is to make each citizen capable of contributing to the state that individual capacity which makes him the most useful. Children, as well as young men and women, are also to be trained in gymnastics and in warlike activities, to provide both for physical fitness and for the security of the city.

[2]Thomas Campanella, *The Defense of Galileo* (Introduction by Grant McColley) *Smith College Studies in History,* 22:xii, April-July, 1937.

Campanella felt that evil had its source in self-love. Communism, he felt, eliminates self-love, since self-love comes mostly from the private ownership of property, *i.e.*, property such as a home, a wife, and children. Hence, the Solarians care little about the family and about private possessions. Men and women, Campanella believed, belong to the state. All the work and study they do, is also part and parcel of the state. The ideal state, he felt, is one which is established for the promotion of the individual, as well as the collective good of all its citizens.

In 1626, Campanella was freed from prison into the custody of the Pope. With the Pope's protection, he was made fully free in 1629. Since Campanella had such great allegiance to the Pope, and to the Church of Rome, the question has often been raised as to whether *City of the Sun* was simply a dream, or whether it was really a sketch for the city of Naples when, and if, she became a free city. This is, however, one of the most famous of utopian works, and Campanella's most characteristic work. As Negley and Patrick point out: "It reveals his polemical nature, his grandiose schemes, his paradoxical fusion of nationalism and mysticism and his indefatigable ingenuity and learning."[3]

CITY OF THE SUN – Thomas Campanella*

A Genoese sea-captain, who has wandered over the world, carries on a dialogue with his host, the Grand Master of the Knights Hospitallers, in which he tells about his experiences in the City of the Sun, in Taprobane, which was found "immediately under the equator." He tells how the Solarians entertained him, explained to him their social institutions and their system of education, and allowed him to observe their theories in practice.

G.M. – I pray you, worthy hero, explain to me their whole system of government; for I am anxious to hear it.

Capt. – The great ruler among them is a priest whom they call by the name Hoh, though we should call him Metaphysic. He is head over all, in temporal and spiritual matters, and all business and lawsuits are settled by him, as the supreme authority. Three princes of equal power – viz., Pon, Sin and Mor – assist him, and these in our tongue we should call Power, Wisdom and Love. To Power belongs the care of all matters relating to war and peace. He attends

---

[3]Glenn Negley and J. Max Patrick, *The Quest for Utopia* (New York: Henry Schuman, 1952), p. 315.

*Thomas Campanella, *City of the Sun* (in *Ideal Empires and Republics*. London: M. Walter Dunne, 1901), pp. 278-281, 290-292, 293-294. This work was published for the first time in 1602.

*to the military arts, and next to Hoh, he is ruler in every affair of a
warlike nature. He governs the military magistrates and the soldiers,
and has the management of the munitions, the fortifications, the
storming of places, the implements of war, the armories, the smiths
and workmen connected with matters of this sort.*

*But Wisdom is the ruler of the liberal arts, of mechanics, of all
sciences with their magistrates and doctors, and of the discipline of
the schools. As many doctors as there are, are under his control.
There is one doctor who is called Astrologus, a second, Cos-
mographus; a third, Arthmeticus; a fourth, Geometra, a fifth,
Historiographus; a sixth, Poeta; a seventh, Logicus, an eighth,
Rhetor; a ninth, Grammaticus; a tenth, Medicus; an eleventh,
Physiologus; a twelth, Politicus; a thirteenth, Moralis. They have but
one book, which they call Wisdom, and in it all the sciences are
written with conciseness and marvelous fluency of expression. This
they read to the people after the custom of the Pythagoreans. It is
Wisdom who causes the exterior and interior, the higher and lower
walls of the city to be adorned with the finest pictures, and to have
all the sciences painted upon them in an admirable manner. On the
walls of the temple and on the dome, which is let down when the
priest gives an address, lest the sounds of his voice, being scattered,
should fly away from his audience, there are pictures of stars in their
different magnitudes, with the powers and motions of each, expressed separately in three little verses.*

*On the interior wall of the first circuit all the mathematical
figures are conspicuously painted – figures more in number than
Archimedes or Euclid discovered, marked symmetrically, and with
the explanation of them neatly written and contained each in a little
verse. There are definitions and propositions, etc., etc. On the
exterior convex wall is first an immense drawing of the whole earth,
given at one view. Following upon this, there are tablets setting forth
for every separate country the customs both public and private, the
laws, the origins and the power of the inhabitants; and the alphabets
the different people use can be seen above that of the City of the
Sun.*

*On the inside of the second circuit, that is to say of the second
ring of buildings, paintings of all kinds of precious and common
stones, of minerals and metals are seen; and a little piece of the metal
itself is also there with an apposite explanation in two small verses
for each metal or stone. On the outside are marked all the seas,
rivers, lakes, and streams which are on the face of the earth; as are
also the wines and the oils and the different liquids, with the sources
from which the last are extracted, their qualities and strength. There*

are also vessels built into the wall above the arches, and these are full of liquids from one to three-hundred years old, which cure all diseases. Hail and snow, storms and thunder, and whatever else takes place in the air, are represented with suitable figures and little verses. The inhabitants even have the art of representing in stone all the phenomena of the air, such as the wind, rain, thunder, the rainbow, etc..

On the interior of the third circuit all the different families of trees and herbs are depicted, and there is a live specimen of each plant in earthenware vessels placed upon the outer partition of the arches. With the specimens there are explanations as to where they were first found, what are their powers and natures, and resemblances to celestial things and to metals: to parts of the human body and to things in the sea, and also as to their use in medicine, etc. On the exterior wall are all the races of fish found in rivers, lakes and seas, and their habits and values, and ways of breeding, training and living, the purposes for which they exist in the world, and their uses to man. Further, their resemblances to celestial and terrestrial things, produced both by nature and art, are so given that I was astonished when I saw a fish which was like a bishop, one like a chain, another like a garment, a fourth like a nail, a fifth like a star, and others like images of those things existing among us, the relation in each case being completely manifest. There are sea urchins to be seen, and the purple shellfish and mussels; and whatever the watery world possesses worthy of being known is there fully shown in marvelous characters of painting and drawing.

On the fourth interior wall all the different kinds of birds are painted, with their natures, sizes, customs, colors, manner of living, etc.; and the only real phoenix is possessed by the inhabitants of this city. On the exterior are shown all the races of creeping animals, serpents, dragons and worms; the insects, the flies, gnats, beetles, etc., in their different states, strength, venoms and uses, and a great deal more than you or I can think of.

On the fifth interior they have all the larger animals of the earth, as many in number as would astonish you. We indeed know not the thousandth part of them, for on the exterior wall also a great many of immense size are also portrayed. To be sure, of horses alone, how great a number of breeds there is and how beautiful are the forms there cleverly displayed.

On the sixth interior are painted all the mechanical arts, with the several instruments for each and their manner of use among different nations. Alongside the dignity of such is placed, and their several inventors are named. But on the exterior all the inventors in science, in warfare, and in law are represented. There I saw Moses, Osiris, Jupiter, Mercury, Lycurgus, Pompilius, Pythagoras, Zamolxis, Solon, Charondas, Phoroneus, with very many others. They even have Mahomet, whom nevertheless they hate as a false and sordid legislator. In the most dignified position I saw a representation of Jesus Christ and of the twelve Apostles, whom they considered very worthy and hold to be great. Of the representations of men, I perceived Caesar, Alexander, Pyrrhus and Hannibal in the highest place; and other very renowned heroes in peace and war,especially Roman heroes, were painted in lower positions, under the galleries. And when I asked with astonishment whence they had obtained our history, they told me that among them there was a knowledge of all languages, and that by perseverence they continually send explorers and ambassadors over the whole earth, who learn thoroughly the customs, forces, rule, and histories of the nations, bad and good alike. These they apply all to their own republic, and with this they are well pleased. I learned that cannon and typography were invented by the Chinese before we knew of them. There are magistrates, who announce the meaning of the pictures, and boys are accustomed to learn all the sciences, without toil and as if for pleasure; but in the way of history only until they are ten years old.

. . . .

G. M. — Tell me about their children.

Capt. — When their women have brought forth children, they suckle and rear them in temples set apart for all. They give milk for two years or more as the physician orders. After that time the weaned child is given into the charge of the mistresses, if it is a female, and to the masters, if it is a male. And then with other young children they are pleasantly instructed in the alphabet, and in the knowledge of the pictures, and in running, walking and wrestling; also in the historical drawings, and in languages; and they are adorned with a suitable garment of different colors. After their sixth year they are taught natural science, and then the mechanical sciences. The men who are weak in intellect are sent to farms, and when they have become more proficient some of them are received into the state. And those of the same age and born under the same constellation are especially like one another in strength and in appearance, and hence arises much lasting concord in the state, these men honoring one another with mutual love and help. Names are given to them by Metaphysicus, and that not by chance but designedly, and according to each one's peculiarity, as was the custom among the ancient Romans. Wherefore one is called Beautiful (Pulcher), another Big-nosed (Naso), another the Fat-legged (Cranipes), another Crooked (Torvus), another Lean (Macer), and so on. But when they have become very skilled in their professions and done any great deed in war or in time of peace, a cognomen from art is given to them, such as Beautiful the great painter (Pulcher, Pictor Magnus), the golden one (Aureus), the excellent one (Excellens), or the strong (Strenuus); or from their deeds, such as Naso the Brave (Nason Fortis), or the cunning, or the great, or very great conqueror; or from the enemy any one has overcome, Africanus, Asiaticus, Etruscus; or if any one has overcome Manfred or Tortelius, he is called Macer Manfred or Tortelius, and so on. All these cognomens are added by the higher magistrates, and very often with a crown suitable to the deed or art, and with the flourish of music. For gold and silver is reckoned of little value among them except as material for their vessels and ornaments, which are common to all.

G. M. − Tell me, I pray you, is there no jealousy among them or disappointment to that one who has not been elected to a magistracy, or to any other dignity to which he aspires?

Capt. − Certainly not. For no one wants either necessaries or luxuries. Moreover, the race is managed for the good of the commonwealth and not of private individuals, and the magistrates must be obeyed. They deny what we hold − viz., that it is natural to man to recognize his offspring and to educate them, and to use his wife and house and children as his own. For they say that children are bred for the preservation of the species and not for individual pleasure, as St. Thomas also asserts. Therefore the breeding of children has reference to the commonwealth and not to individuals, except in so far as they are constituents of the commonwealth. And since individuals for the most part bring forth children wrongly and educate them wrongly, they consider that they remove destruction from the state, and, therefore, for this reason, with most sacred fear, they commit the education of the children, who as it were are the element of the republic, to the care of magistrates; for the safety of the community is not that of a few.

. . . .

Every man who, when he is told off to work, does his duty, is considered very honorable. It is not the custom to keep slaves. For they are enough, and more than enough, for themselves. But with us, alas! it is not so. In Naples there exist seventy thousand souls, and out of these scarcely ten or fifteen thousand do any work, and they are always lean from overwork and are getting weaker every day. The rest become a prey to idleness, avarice, ill-health, lasciviousness, usury and other vices, and contaminate and corrupt very many families by holding them in servitude for their own use, by keeping them in poverty and slavishness, and by imparting to them their own vices. Therefore public slavery ruins them; useful works, in the field, in military service, and in arts, except those which are debasing, are not cultivated, the few who do practice them doing so with much aversion. But in the City of the Sun, while duty and work is distributed among all, it only falls to each one to work for about four hours every day. The remaining hours are spent in learning joyously, in debating, in reading, in reciting, in writing, in walking, in exercising the mind and body, and with play. They allow no game which is played while sitting, neither the single die nor dice, nor chess, nor others like these. But they play with the ball, with the sack, with the hoop, with wrestling, with hurling at the stake. They say, moreover, that grinding poverty renders men worthless, cunning, sulky, thievish, insidious, vagabonds, liars, false witnesses, etc.; and that wealth makes them insolent, proud, ignorant, traitors, assumers of what they know not, deceivers, boasters, wanting in affection, slanderers, etc. But with them all the rich and poor together make up the community. They are rich because they want nothing, poor because they possess nothing; and consequently they are not slaves to circumstances, but circumstances serve them. And on this point they strongly recommend the religion of the Christians, and especially the life of the Apostles.

Chapter Four

JOHANN VALENTIN ANDREAE
AND *CHRISTIANOPOLIS*

Johann Valentin Andreae was a son of the Renaissance. In his writings he exemplifies the great movement for exploration and creation, which was so typical of the period. Unheard-of continents and new races were being discovered by Spanish and Portuguese explorers. Men were seeking changes, even in the established order of things, such as Luther's questioning of the authority of the church. Professor Held points to this spirit of the times when he says:

> *The Renaissance marks the time when men's thoughts were called to the subject of reform. The practical turn given by Humanism away from sophistical, disputing, dreamy abstractions, towards the affairs of life; the enlightenment of the world, spiritually and mentally, due to the revival of learning; and especially the discovery of the western world, all tended to give man and society a new impetus – a swelling, crowding, longing desire for a fuller, freer, larger life.* [1]

Christianopolis, the story of a newly found country with reformed ideas not only appealed to the mind of the Renaissance but has also influenced later thinkers and writers. It is considered the form after which Bacon's *New Atlantis* and Gott's *Nova Solyma* are patterned. It also influenced Comenius, who considered himself a pupil of Andreae.

Andreae set his utopian society in the South Seas. In *Christianopolis* he pictures himself as wrecked in a mythical ship named Phantasy and afterwards thrown up as the sole survivor on an uncharted island known as Caphar Salama. Here he found an unknown race of people who tested his virtue and intelligence before showing him their city with its advanced methods. After satisfactorily proving that he is a good Christian, he is allowed entrance. He finds four hundred people living in a rectangular enclosure about seven hundred feet long and almost as wide. This enclosure is surrounded by a deep moat.

[1] Johann Valentin Andreae, *Christianopolis* (translated with Introduction by Felix Emil Held), (New York: Oxford University Press, 1916), Introduction, p. 4.

The government of *Christianopolis* is a triumvirate, and is essentially the same as that of a republic, with various groups having representation according to vocations like the guild towns of the Middle Ages. There is also a group of experts in various fields, who cooperate with the council in advancing the policies of the government.

Everything in *Christianopolis* is carefully planned. There is no money, but goods are distributed by a State Economist whose duty is to see that everyone receives an equal proportion of goods. There are few working hours, and there are also many vacation periods, which are designed to act as a stimulus to work. All work, even manual labor, is held in esteem as Andreae strongly believed that manual labor complemented intellectual activity.

Religion is the keystone of Caphar Salama. Andreae presents us essentially with a theocratic community. He felt that religion was under attack in the world, such as he saw in Geneva, and it was in such a place as this that an honest Christian could really find refuge. Everything on this island was done under the eye of those who held deeply felt religious principles, and everything was believed by them to represent an attempt to create a sort of heaven on earth. However, the religious convictions of the author were often threatening and antihumanistic, as Berneri points out:

> *One would feel more attracted to* Christianopolis *if Andreae's religious principles had allowed him more understanding for human feelings, as if man's nature were allowed to express itself without being suspected of falling, at every moment, into the snares of Satan. But we are reminded at every other line of the wickedness of man. . .*
>
> *Throughout his utopia one feels that his love of man inclined him to trust them as sensible beings capable of going about their lives in a reliable and honest way, but his religion told him that man is wicked and has to be carefully guided, preached to, and, if necessary, threatened, to be kept away from sin. That is why his ideal city is a curious combination of free guilds and religious tyranny, of personal responsibility and of complete submission to religion.* [2]

Andreae puts great value upon the development of character in *Christianopolis*. He felt that this should be one of the prime purposes of education; and there were educational experts in *Christianopolis* whose sole concern was the development of character in their pupils.

[2]Marie Louise Berneri, *Journey Through Utopia* (London: Routledge and Kegan Paul, Ltd., 1950), pp. 106-107.

These men became the arbiters of truth and morality in the state, and their role is considered by Andreae to be an extremely important one.

In this utopia, great care is given to the construction and appearance of the school buildings, as well as to the choice of teachers. Both girls and boys are given training early, and when they reach their sixth year they belong to the state, continuing their education in special boarding schools apart from their family.

Andreae conceived of this school as being divided into eight departments of education. The first is the school of arts. After suitable progress in this department, the student proceeds to the departments of logic, metaphysics, and theosophy, and in turn, to the departments of mathematics, music, astronomy, natural philosophy, ethics, and theology. Besides these, there are two additional departments, dealing with medicine and jurisprudence. Andreae also approved of the formation of a "college" or society which would permit men of learning to gather together for the purpose of carrying out research. It was this idea which contributed in part to the development of the Royal Society in England.

Andreae saw, as he points out in the beginning of *Christianopolis,* two classes existing in society: those who constantly admire and defend present conditions, and those who wish for improvement. Andreae was decidedly one of the latter. He was no mere visionary, but one who was engaged in the use of his utopian ideas as rules for practical reform. When he was called to Calw as teacher and minister, he tried to establish in part such a social system as he had outlined in *Christianopolis.* His reforms at Calw included the founding of mutual protective associations among the workers, as well as improvements in the system of education.

Andreae was a great admirer of Martin Luther. He felt, however, that a reformation was needed not only in religion but in society as a whole. The larger reforms which he envisioned depended a great deal upon a major overhaul in education, and thus *Christianopolis,* as well as his *Theophilus,* describe the manner after which an educational reform should pattern itself. Andreae was impatient for men to move ahead — to seek communion with God on earth by achieving a perfect Christian society. He felt that by developing a society in which man's goodness could be tapped, we would be approaching the divine injunction of God, which called for all men to love one another as brothers.

CHRISTIANOPOLIS – Johann Valentin Andreae*

In an introduction which is strongly allegorical, our hero, a stranger to tyranny, false art, and hypocrisy, sets sail on a ship named Phantasy in search of enlightenment and a peaceful land. After some sailing, storms of envy and calumny suddenly rise up and sink the ship. Our hero is washed up on the island of Caphar Salama, where he is interrogated by three officials who guard against tramps and beggars, people with poor characters, and those with inadequate scholarship. After obtaining their approval, he is shown the futuristic city of Christianopolis, together with its advanced policies in education.

THE COLLEGE

Now is the time when we approach the innermost shrine of the city which you would rightly call the center of activity of the state. It is square, two-hundred and seventy feet on the outside, a hundred and ninety feet on the inside, bounded by four corner towers and intersected by as many others, opposite each other and enclosed by a double line of gardens. There are in the whole building four stories, rising respectively to a height of twelve, eleven, ten, and nine feet; and the towers extend eight feet more even above these. Toward the market-place, on the inside, there is an open porch, very attractive with its seventy-two columns. Here religion, justice, and learning have their abode, and theirs is the control of the city; and eloquence has been given them as an interpreter. Never have I seen so great an amount of human perfection collected into one place, and you will confess the same when you shall have heard a description of the sights. And yet I often wonder what people mean who separate and disjoin their best powers, the joining of which might render them blessed as far as this may be on earth. There are those who would be considered religious, who throw off all things human; there are some who are pleased to rule, though without any religion at all; learning makes a great noise, flattering now this one, now that, yet applauding itself most. What finally may the tongue do except provoke God, confuse men, and destroy itself? So there would seem to be a need of cooperation which only Christianity can give — Christianity which conciliates God with men and unites men together, so that they have pious thoughts, do good deeds, know the truth, and finally die happily to live eternally. Let us then cooperate once lest we be separated for eternity.

*Johann Valentin Andreae, *Christianopolis* (translated by Felix Emil Held), (New York: Oxford University Press, 1916), pp. 173-174, 186-187, 205-210. This work was originally published in 1619.

THE DIRECTOR OF LEARNING

The third of the triumvirs, Abida, has the sphere of human learning. I found him, contrary to expectation, without haughtiness or laziness. All about the man was kindly, nothing crabbed. It was thought there was little he did not know; yet in his modesty he professed an ignorance of all things. There was lack of nothing except, among his colleagues, the decorations of titles. He always said that the man who studied as a disciple under the direction of the Holy Spirit, had accomplished something. When I inquired as to the sum of all learning, he mentioned Christ and Him crucified, saying that all things pointed toward Him. He seemed at one time condemning the earth and praising the heavens; and then again he seemed to be estimating the earth highly, and the heavens as of less value. For he insisted that a close examination of the earth would bring about a proper appreciation of the heavens, and when the value of the heavens had been found, there would be a contempt of the earth. At the same time he entirely disapproved of all that literature which did not bring one nearer to Christ; if it tended to separate one from Christ, he cursed it. He centered all importance in the church, which had been tossed about so many thousands of years upon the world-ocean; to the church were due, he said, all tongues, all history, all reasoning, all signs of nature, all arts of the heavens; then finally one might expect the gift of blessed eternity. Only Christians have knowledge, but it is of God. All remaining things are foolishness, because they come out of one's self. These facts surprised me greatly when I heard all things made light of which among others are praised highly. But I was convinced when I remembered why we are born into this world, namely, to enjoy Christ, our absolute necessity, our invaluable gain. But when it falls our lot to die, woe to the miserable literature which had fed us for a few days on smoke! Arise, thou sacred science which shall explain to us Christ, that we may here learn things that are not to be unlearned, but to be increased and extended into all ages!

. . . .

THE DEPARTMENTS OF LEARNING

When I had been conducted from this place (The Mathematics Laboratory) to a higher floor, I saw a school, roomy and beautiful beyond expectation, divided into eight lecture halls where the youths, the most valuable asset of the republic, are molded and trained to God, nature, reason, and public safety. For if injunctions are given to individuals to bring up their children excellently, why should they not do the same for the commonwealth that the best method of education and instruction be entered in upon? For this most important of all duties they have furnished this very elaborate place, that they might thus declare their love and care for these, their children of greatest promise, and that they might, as it were, merit future hapiness in advance. All this is not after the infamous example of the world. For when the world seems to love her children most of all, she often shuts them up in some out of the way, unhealthy, and even dirty prison, where they are brought into contact with filth and become accustomed to such jails. Here all is open, sunny, and happy, so that with the sight of pictures, even, they attract the children, fashion the minds of the boys and girls, and advise the youths. They are not baked in summer not frozen in winter; they are not disturbed by noise nor frightened because of loneliness. Whatever is elsewhere given over to luxury and leisure of palaces is here devoted to honorable recreation and pursuits, an investment that is nowhere more satisfactory or better paying. For even as the earth when well cultivated returns with interest what has been entrusted to it, so youth when steeped in the lifeblood of the republic and impelled to a joyous harvest, pays back everything with usury. This is the summit of happiness, to be able with one and the same effort to preserve the safety of the republic and the adjustment of the future life, so that the children which we bear here we may find to our satisfaction have been born for the heavens as much as for the earth.

. . . .

THE TEACHERS

Their instructors are not men from the dregs of human society nor such as are useless for other occupations, but the choice of all the citizens, persons whose standing in the republic is known and who very often have access to the highest positions in the state. For surely, no one can properly take care of the youth unless he is also able to discharge the duties of state; and he who succeeds with the youth, has thereby already established his right to serve in governmental affairs. The teachers are well advanced in years and they are especially remarkable for their pursuit of four virtues: dignity, integrity, activity, and generosity. For if they are not successful with their scholars and disciples and are not highly valued by the public; if they do not excel others in reverence toward God, uprightness toward their neighbor, and in firmness and moderation in their own lives, and are not an example in virtue; if they do not give evidence of skill, wisdom and the highest power of judgment for instruction and education, as well as a recognition of the crises in the natures of their pupils; if they do not prefer to spur their charges on as free agents with kindness, courteous treatment, and a liberal discipline rather than with threats, blows, and like sternness; if these are not their ideals as instructors, then the citizens of Christianopolis do not deem them worthy of organizing this miniature republic, the successor of the greater, nor of being intrusted with the very substance of their future safety. As they succeed so well in keeping up a condition at all times resembling a state government, they can with good grace warn others, not lightly to expose the very valuable, supple, and active youth to the vilest, most vicious, insipid, and coarsest men, merely because such may be had more cheaply. Under such care children are brought up to waste their parents' goods, not by measures but by whole bins; and perhaps later on they in turn leave behind them children even worse than themselves.

. . . .

THE PUPILS

Now it will be well to mention who the pupils are and of what sort. All the children of citizens in general, children of both sexes, are taken into training. When they have completed their sixth year the parents give them over to the state, not without prayers and pious vows. The pupils are divided into three classes: the children, the youth, and the mature. Here they eat and sleep, and receive mental and physical training. The more numerous their offspring, the happier the parents are, for they then lack nothing; from this one fact it can be seen how unrestrictedly the citizens live. No parent gives closer or more careful attention to his children than is given here, for the most upright preceptors, men as well as women, are placed over them. Moreover, they can visit their children, even unseen by them, as often as they have leisure. As this is an institution for the public good it is managed very agreeably as a common charge for all the citizens. They see to it carefully that the food is appetizing and wholesome, that the couches and beds are clean and comfortable, and that the clothes and attire of the whole body are clean. The pupils wash often and use linen towels for drying. The hair is also combed to prevent anything unclean from collecting. If diseases of the skin or body are contracted, the individuals in question are cared for in good time; and to avoid the spreading of the infection, they are quarantined. They do these things as diligently as the world attends to its duties neglectfully. For there is no need of my mentioning here the dirtiness of the schools, the uncleanness of food and beds, and the rudeness of those in charge toward the scholars; inasmuch as those who have suffered these indignities bear witness not so much with cries and complaints, as with bodies feeble throughout all life, for this very reason.

. . . .

THE NATURE OF INSTRUCTION

Their first and highest exertion is to worship God with a pure and faithful soul; the second, to strive toward the best and most chaste morals; the third, to cultivate the mental powers — an order, reversed by the world, if any thought of God still remains among the inhabitants of the latter. Moreover, they feel themselves dedicated to God, by the law of their birth into this world, as well as by the agency of their parents. They begin their study not with some absurd deposition, that is, some prelude of foolishness, but with earnest prayers. From this they proceed through the fixed stages of those beginning, those advancing, and those who have completed the course, with high-sounding titles, it is true; but they unlearn these easily on growing more mature. The titles are a great incentive to the degrees, as a noble mind is raised by praise while it is stimulated by a slight disgrace. There is need of strict uprightness on the part of those who give the titles, lest while they are thus playing they should haply trifle with the youth. This is where much wrong is done in other places, and all the more so because it is not without gain and loss. For to accept pay and to sell the ignorant to the state is certainly not just. Punishments are inflicted with fasting and work; if there is need, with whipping; in extreme cases, though rarely, by imprisonment. The young men have their study periods in the morning, the girls in the afternoon; and matrons as well as learned men are their instructors. I do not know why this sex, which is naturally no less teachable, is elsewhere excluded from literature. The rest of their time is devoted to manual training and domestic art and science, as each one's occupation is assigned according to his natural inclination. When they have vacant time, they are permitted to engage in honorable physical exercises either in the open spaces of the town or in the field. Here they may contest in running or wrestling, they may play ball, or even exercise with weapons; or, if they are old enough, they may break horses. You will approve of all these, if you do not forget that moderation and careful supervision are required in everything.

Chapter Five

SAMUEL GOTT AND NOVA SOLYMA

A dispute that has not yet reached its climax is the one over who is the author of *Nova Solyma*. In a historical introduction to the 1902 edition, the Reverend Walter Begley claims emphatically that John Milton is the true author of this work. Begley supports his arguments by comparing the ideas on music, religion, and poetry in *Nova Solyma* to other works by Milton. He ends by saying that his strongest argument is the fact that Milton had a penchant for literary mysticism and the concealment of authorship.

Several prominent literary critics have disputed this claim, however. In 1904 J. Churton Collins[1] pointed out that there is no record in Milton's journals of such a work as this having been written, nor have the careful contemporary biographers of Milton recorded it. Collins points out that, among other things, Milton's educational views as found in his *Tractate* differ markedly from those found in *Nova Solyma*.

> *The one is chiefly concerned with the training of young children, the other ignores it. The one subordinates intellectual to moral discipline, the other subordinates moral to intellectual. The one recognizes the importance of equipping young citizens for mercantile and mechanical pursuits, the other turns from such aims with aristocratic contempt. The one attaches the greatest importance to composition both in prose and verse, the other discourages such exercises. In Nova Solyma music is ignored as an educational instrument; in the Tractate the greatest stress is laid upon its importance.* [2]

The confusion of authorship was somewhat enhanced, Jones[3] believes, by the fact that Samuel Gott and John Milton both left Cambridge in the same year. Since they were contemporaries, it was an easy matter for critics to assign an unknown work of this stature

[1]J. Churton Collins, "Miltonic Myths and Their Authors," *The National Review*, July, 1904, pp. 768-785.
[2]*Ibid.*, p. 781.
[3]Stephen K. Jones, "The Authorship of 'Nova Solyma'," *The Library*, Third Series, 1:225-238, July, 1910.

to Milton. Gott was, and still is, a relatively unknown author. His name is not found in ordinary biographical dictionaries, and his only other known work is an obscure one entitled *An Essay on the True Happiness of Man,* published in 1650.

Jones, Collins, and Patrick [4] are convinced that Gott is the true author of this work, due to the fact that there is some reference to it made in the personal journals in which he kept accounts. Though there are some similarities to Milton's views, the fact that Milton, a careful recorder, kept no evidence of his authorship, is a damaging point.

Gott, from what little evidence we have, seems to have been a very erudite scholar. He read widely in Latin, and appears to have also been a Hebrew scholar. He was a very religious person, and as Patrick expresses it, "His views are those of a liberal orthodox Puritan."[5]

Gott expresses in *Nova Solyma* the Puritan view that it was necessary for man to justify the ways of man to God. He thus promotes a high degree of individualism, and believed that it was up to the individual to achieve his own salvation. The winning of salvation, Gott believed, could not be achieved by or through the state, but only through a personal religious experience in which the individual achieved real union with the deity.

It is significant that Gott's utopia is called New Jerusalem, and is peopled by highly intelligent and far-sighted Jews, for the influence of Hebraic knowledge was an important aspect of seventeenth-century thought. This attitude was part and parcel of the religious fervor which then existed in Europe, especially in England, where the Bible was undergoing serious study by scholars who preferred to read it in the original Hebrew. The Hebraic language was diligently studied by many students at Cambridge and Oxford, and many of the early Puritans who settled in America during the seventeenth-century, such as Richard Mather and John Cotton, were Hebrew scholars. The Reverend D. de Sola Pool traces a direct relationship between Hebrew learning and many of the ideas of the early Puritans who flourished in England before sailing for America and other places.[6] It is quite possible that Gott's own interest in Hebraic scholarship led him to an acceptance of the same ideals.

---

[4] J. Max Patrick, "Puritanism and Poetry: Samuel Gott," *University of Toronto Quarterly,* January, 1939, pp. 211-226.

[5] *Ibid.,* p. 216.

[6] Rev. D. de Sola Pool, *Hebrew Learning Among the Puritans of New England Prior to 1700,* Publications of the American Jewish Historical Society, No. 20, 1911.

Nova Solyma, unlike Plato's *Republic* and Campanella's *City of the Sun,* is notable for the high regard Gott has for the individual to make his own decisions in life.

> *His ideal realm, Nova Solyma, is noteworthy in utopian literature for the absence of constant interference with the individual by the state. He advocates few reforms; he willingly accepts the class structures of society. Though his educational ideas are liberal, they preserve these class distinctions. His greatest desire is to foster a moral or religious tendency in all departments of human life.*[7]

Gott was a proponent of the view that "the state that governs least, governs best," and believed that the state should interfere with the life of a person as little as possible. He believed that the laws of both God and man were kept best when individuals did not obey them out of fear, or because of external compunction, but rather because they saw it was in their own best interests to do so. We see this same attitude exemplified in education where he believed that vices such as obstinacy and pride were handled more effectively when the individual was taught to exercise voluntary control, rather than having to obey outside rules. He therefore suggests prizes, rather than moral precepts, as a means for overcoming such bad habits. When the ability to exercise voluntary control is lacking, however, the Jews of Nova Solyma are not hesitant about forcing one toward the desired goals, by whipping if necessary.

We find a very high regard for education in *Nova Solyma.* It is noteworthy to point out that the Reverend Mr. Begley found teachers held in little esteem at the time of the writing of this book, yet Gott restores them to what might be termed, "a lost prestige."

> *For the Jews of Nova Solyma do not hold schoolmasters in contempt, as so many other nations do, nor do they class them simply as superior servants, who have to see chiefly that the children are kept safe, and do not get into mischief. On the contrary, they are classed with the chief magistrates of the nation, and especially are those schoolmasters held in honor who have the charge of the young and untrained, for they are invested with the Order of the Sun, appropriately enough too, for the sun is the dispeller of all darkness, and renders possible the active duties of life.*[8]

[7]J. Max Patrick, "Puritanism and Poetry: Samuel Gott," *University of Toronto Quarterly,* January, 1939, p. 217.

[8]Samuel Gott, *Nova Solyma* (translated by the Rev. Walter Begley, and erroneously ascribed to John Milton), (New York: Charles Scribner's Sons, 1902), p. 234.

The first stage of one's education in *Nova Solyma* begins, however, not in the classroom, but in the home. Children do not begin to take formalized instruction until they reach ten years of age, and during this time that they are in the home they are to learn such important things as kindness from the mother and firmness from the father. Gott was a strong believer in the preservation of the family unit, and hoped that children would seek the advice and counsel of their parents during their entire lives.

The second stage of education begins when the child enters into the public academy. At this time, he is carefully studied in order to learn his personality, as well as his preferences in subject-matter. By this means, it is hoped that a psychological insight can be achieved into the character of the individual, so that he can be better guided and directed on an educational process that will bring out his full potentialities. Each pupil's education is thus distinct in that it is tailor-made to his own talents and capacities. It is also geared for placing an individual in the position in the state which best befits him and hopefully, thus providing for his future happiness.

Students are taught grammar and mathematics, as well as Greek, Latin, and Hebrew. Some foreign languages are also taught, particularly of those nations in which Nova Solyma has mercantile interests. Students may also specialize in certain fields, such as writing or the study of rhetoric, which is held in great esteem. Gott also believed, as Plato did, that education should not consist merely in the training of the mind, and therefore we find an equal attention given to such athletic endeavors as running, swimming, riding, drilling, and archery.

Students who have obtained their degree in arts and have shown themselves capable of going on to more advanced work are permitted to do so. They may study in such fields as philosophy, theology, medicine, and law. For these studies only the best professors are engaged, who receive the highest salaries of those in the teaching profession. The less gifted students are not neglected either, for they are also given additional studies which will allow them to rise "to the full height of their capacity."

Religion in *Nova Solyma,* as in *Christianopolis,* plays a very significant role in education, as in everything else. All children are taught to worship God, and inducing the religious habit of mind is considered the first and chief care of education. For Gott, as well as for Andreae, religion is the sacred glue which keeps all of the diverse parts of the society bound together into one harmonious whole.

NOVA SOLYMA - Samuel Gott*

As the Jews have finally been converted, a new Jerusalem, Nova Solyma, an ideal city, has been created, and two Cambridge students, Eugenius and Politian, set out to visit it. They discover a person named Joseph, of this city, who has been robbed by some brigands. Joseph thus becomes their guide to Nova Solyma and takes them by horseback to visit his home. They are welcomed by his father, Jacob, who bids them to remain as his guests. In the following selections, Joseph and one of the schoolmasters at the university, named Alphaeus, explain to them the purposes and methods of education in this land of Zion.

"We try to improve by art and culture in every way the gifts of body and mind with which kindly Nature endows our race, in order that our children, both by their natural ability and the formative care they receive when young, may strive onwards to the acme of human perfection. We accustom by degrees the frames of younger members to endure hardness, subject to the doctor's advice, and we boast of it as one of the best signs of our kind consideration for them, that they have been prepared for all the changes and chances of mortal life from their very cradle. For it is a simple matter of experience that the children of the poor, brought up with the greatest frugality, and in clothing of the scantiest, leaving them exposed to every inclemency, yet turn out healthier and of better constitution than those who are delicately and luxuriously brought up. As soon as they can stand on their feet and begin to walk, they are taught to do so gracefully and firmly, for a slovenly and ridiculous gait, whether it may proceed from an early formed bad habit or from an accidental cause, is always amenable to careful correction, and, with the exception of the true beauty that Nature sometimes gives to the face and figure, there is nothing more pleasing and dignified than a seemly and distinguished action of the body in walking; whether it be natural or acquired matters not, but it must be unaffected. We add too, as part of this training, those gestures and movements of the whole body which are most becoming; and after that we practice running, for swiftness of foot is not only a most useful quality for its own sake, but it also is good for the lungs and staying powers of our youths, who in this art are not a whit inferior to the barbarians, who are used to the roughest ground. Dancing, swimming, archery, and such like pursuits receive attention, and it is scarcely credible what progress is made in these by constant practice, so that what is a record with other nations is with us quite usual, especially in really

*Samuel Gott, *Nova Solyma* (translated by the Rev. Walter Begley, and erroneously attributed to John Milton), (New York: Charles Scribner's Sons, 1902), pp. 90-96, 235-239. This work was originally published in London in 1648.

useful arts. For whatever we hear, on good authority, is able to be accomplished by men, this we urge our youth to attempt, with this saving clause, that these trials of strength should be gradually increasing and never excessive, lest by too violent exertion there be danger of present strain or bad effects in after years. And verily I think the body is worthy of such care and trouble, as it is most closely connected with the vital principle, and on its soundness and good health depend most of the duties of life. And thus we do not, like the Europeans, regard culture as consisting mainly in the accomplishments and training of the mind, and take hardly any account of the body, nor yet, like the barbarians, do we dispense with all mental training and book-learning because we share their high opinion of a strong and enduring frame. We follow the glorious example of the old Greeks and Romans, and pay our regard to both mind and body. The earliest faults that show themselves in children are passion and an overreadiness to cry and yell, and afterwards obstinacy, pride, and envy. These are the vices we first of all try to master. We foster a voluntary habit of endurance and good temper, more by contrivance and the giving of prizes than by moral precepts. We do not allow anything to be wrung from us by tears — rather any method than that. Obstinacy is made to yield to fear and reverence. We take great care not to encourage a too haughty temper by any empty flattery or foolish talk. Kindness and liberality are commended; none are allowed to take pleasure in others' misfortunes or to mock at them, whether they be in real life or only, maybe, on the stage. Especially do we try to restrain the violent desires of our nature in the bonds of temperance and chastity. We put special restrictions on eating and sleeping too much; all must rise early and eat what happens to be set before them. Hardly ever do they get the chance of delicacies; but sometimes, to create disgust, we allow them to gorge to repletion.

"By such training good manners can be best formed; nor is this a hard matter if the precautions are taken well in time. In fact, do we not see dogs, fierce and untamable as they are naturally, voluntarily lay aside their savage ways under the constant action of the blow or the caress? Are not colts too, who for three or four years have been allowed to run free in the fields and parks, most difficult to break in without force and management?

"But not only do we check the passions when they wander away from the right road; we are equally zealous in whipping them up when they are sluggish and timid. The drawbacks of nervousness and bashfulness are made good by going much into society and by facing danger. Yet, after all, our highest endeavor is to kindle into

flame the spark of genius that may be latent in each, for we cannot hope that those who only follow the trite and vulgar pursuits of the mob can ever be so fired with enthusiasm as to dare, I will not say do, any truly great and noble act. Meanwhile we season their minds with the salt of soberness and self-restraint, lest by want of it they should fall into the splendid sins of the pagan world.

"We begin the discipline from the earliest childhood, especially at that period when they first learn to talk; and the fact that this is such a laborious and difficult piece of learning clearly points out that the minds of children, who are able to attach a certain meaning to so many different words not in the least suggesting the nature of the objects, are really able to profit by instruction of this kind sooner than we believe. With what learning do you think we first try their budding capacities?"

"With grammar, I suppose," said Eugenius.

"You are right so far," said Jacob; "but we also try them with arithmetic and the simpler mathematics, for it has appeared to us that those sciences which are the least mixed up with the customs of mankind, and have their first principles in the nature of things, and can be tested by the senses, are by far the best adapted to bring out the reasoning powers, and to strengthen the grasp of the youthful mind, always so apt to wander and to lack concentration.

"To the younger boys and the backward ones we give short and simple questions; to the elder and those who are sharp scholars more difficult tasks are assigned. We contrive games also for them where calculation of figures and weights and measures are brought in, and they are not allowed to play in a foolish or thoughtless manner, for we think that the eager desire for a game of this sort in the young and light-hearted affords the very best opportunity to strengthen both their bodies and minds. In fact, hardly any portion of their daily life is allowed to lie fallow, but is so cultivated that each should bring forth the best fruit in due season.

"Above all, we attach importance to the proper exercise of faith and imagination. Shameless and impure acts they are taught to shrink from with horror as from monstrosities and awful portents, and to acknowledge with the highest reverence an Infinite and Invisible Deity. We rank liars with those creatures which have not the use of speech, and treat them as equally unsuited for the society of articulately speaking men. Beginning in this way, our young children are most carefully brought up to worship God and love their country; we instill respect and reverence to parents and elders, and that liberality between brothers which indeed gave occasion to what I am now saying.

"This course goes on till they are about ten; the younger of my two boys is nine, the elder not quite ten yet."

Here Politian raised an objection. *"Although,"* he said, *"I quite understand how you, a chief citizen, can expend very large sums on the education of your children, and that they are quite able to profit by it, yet I think I am right in saying that it is not in the power of every parent so to educate his children, nor is it every child who could so well repay the time and trouble spent."*

"But," proceeded Jacob, *"this education of ours is open to all classes, and is the work our teachers and moralists have handed on to us. Our plan is to have prudent men of experience, who can be questioned and consulted — who are, so to speak, Inspectors and Directors of Education. And besides these, we have public discourses held frequently in all parts of the land, not only of a religious nature, but on ethics, the family life, and such topics. And so, you see, our education gains an entrance to the family circle; and although it cannot be equally successful everywhere, still, if any one is gifted with abilities out of the common, it looks after him and helps his career. Nor is any one with natural endowments of a higher order allowed to remain unnoticed and neglected from the obscurity of his birth, as is so often the case elsewhere.*

"Nor are the less gifted despised on that account, and reckoned unworthy of much educational care; indeed, we use special endeavors in their case, that they may be able at least to rise to the full height of their capacity, and in due course fitly perform their duties to the State. In point of fact, when we, as teachers, look for the highest results and greatest pleasure from our work, we find that it is not so much the very talented that satisfy us, for these, by their short-comings in other matters, often cause far more trouble and offence than do those pupils of less ability, but greater natural goodness and disposition."

. . . .

Then Alphaeus (for that was the name of the master), sitting down in his chair of office, asked them to sit beside him, and thus began:

"We do not take upon us to strike a blow against other methods of study, nor do we superciliously force our foreign students to conform to our national habits; but we maintain that experience and results make it clear that our system, whatever be its peculiarity, is not a failure. The founders of our republic, in their zealous enquiry

how best to establish it on a sound basis, put the education of the rising generation in the very forefront of all means to that end. They held the opinion that good laws, an effective army, and all the other defenses of a State, were of comparatively no avail if obedience and benevolence and the other virtues which tend to the well-being of mankind were not early implanted in the minds of the young; they thought it would not be an easy natural thing for citizens to act for the commonweal unless from their youth up they were accustomed to restrain their natural evil desires, and to learn that habit of mind by which they would willingly, in their own interests, keep inviolate the laws of God and their country, and put the advantage of the republic before any private or personal benefits whatever. Wherefore they spared neither skill nor labor nor expense in properly preparing the ground at this critical period of youth, especially did they bestow every care on this great public school, or academy, intended for the flower of the age, and to be an example for all other teaching institutions in the land. I have now been head of it for twenty years, having had but two predecessors, our duty being to visit and supervise the affiliated schools as well. These schools are in the principal town of each province or district, and they are inspected in order each year by myself and my chief assistants, and I advise where it is needed. And thus the method and character of our teaching is spread throughout the whole country, and any lazy or cramming head-masters are stirred up to better results. Our pupils are either lads of gentle birth, who by their position in life are likely to make a figure in State councils, or else lads of great natural parts and good promise, admitted with the prospect of reaching the like honor. These last, if their means require it, are supported by public scholarships, instituted for that purpose, the funds for which have always been so far faithfully administered. And it has always been no slight recommendation to any candidate for public service or the magisterial office if he has taken his degree with us. Hence we are pretty sure to keep up our numbers, and there is no lack of suitable students, for all who have this ambition of serving the State naturally seek admission here. All this wonderfully dignifies their work, and spurs them on to make progress. There are technical schools as well, and public workshops where the children of the poorer classes are taught the meaner occupations, or, if they show ability, are instructed in the mechanical arts and crafts. Others follow the trades by which they earn their livelihood in a private and more independent manner. The education of all these goes no farther than reading, writing, arithmetic with geometry, and other such studies as are a help to the mechanical arts, for the higher culture is considered out of place in their station of life, and even prejudicial, from its tendency to make the working classes dissatisfied with their humble duties, if once they have tasted the dignified "sweetness and light" of the intellectual life. But as regards morality, military drill, and religious exercises, these are inculcated on all without exception. We consider a beggar no better than a thief, and that they who give alms to such do more harm than good. Our plan is to appoint suitable collectors of charitable contributions, which are prudently distributed to meet real want, and therefore we have a special dislike to beggars as casting a slur on our public charity, and as being the very dregs of the population. Moreover, we cannot understand how those who are in need can be better supported by chance benevolence than by regular collections. We regard trade with much favor; all classes of society engage in it. Merchants and farmers are under no social discredit; it is only the dishonest business people who are despised and disgraced.

"But to return to my pupils and their training here. Our first and chief care is to induce the religious habit of mind, our next to inculcate the ethical duties, and our last care (which others make their first) is a liberal education, both literary and scientific. Our religious training is mainly directed to the feelings of a spiritual character. We do not weary our boys with deep disputations, we do not confuse them with mysteries, nor do we hinder them by casuistic scruples and discouragements.

"Those who intend to take up theology as a profession receive no stricter religious education than their fellow pupils, although they have to attend special divinity classes in their course. But the power and essence of religion, as far as it is conducive to a good and happy life, are hardly anywhere so generally insisted upon with every student as with us, for we hold religion to be the foundation and corner-stone of society, and the great connecting link that holds it together in all its different sections."

Chapter Six

ROBERT OWEN AND A NEW VIEW OF SOCIETY

Margaret Cole, who calls Robert Owen one of the first of the modern utopians, says further, "As soon as he began to think for himself, Owen was a Utopian – a millennialist, who believed that a perfect society could be, and should be attained in a very short space of time."[1] Certainly, if reports which have come down to us about Owen are true, he was a man impatient that his ideas at New Lanark were not put into practice sooner. He complains continuously throughout his autobiography of having to proceed "at a snail's pace."

When one considers what radical changes Owen effected at New Lanark one cannot help marveling at his intelligence and good, plain common sense. Owen was an astute businessman who, with a few others, purchased some cotton mills in New Lanark, Scotland. The cotton mills became a very profitable enterprise, and Owen one of the leading philanthropists of his day. Owen felt that being a businessman was in itself neither enobling or degrading. It was what one did with his wealth that was the important thing.

Owen was one of the first of the British writers to really understand the meaning of the Industrial Revolution and throughout his business career was an ardent enthusiast of new techniques and methods of production. What disturbed him was not the growing technological advance, but the way in which machines and businesses were used to degrade and enslave men. Owen believed that capital should be used to relieve human suffering and to raise the workingman to a higher level in life.

Owen tells in his autobiography of the great difficulties he had to overcome in taking a partnership in the textile mills of New Lanark, Scotland.

> The evil conditions which I had to contend against were the ignorance, superstition, and consequent immoral conduct and bad habits of the great majority of the population; the long day's work

[1]Margaret Cole, *Robert Owen of New Lanark* (New York: Oxford University Press, 1953), p. 72.

which they had to undergo; the inferior qualities and high price of
everything which they had to purchase for their own use; the bad
arrangements in their houses for rearing and training their children
from their birth through infancy and childhood; and their prejudice
against an English manufacturer becoming a hard taskmaster, as they
imagined I was going to be, because they saw I was going to adopt
what they called new-fangled measures.[2]

Owen did indeed adopt many "new-fangled measures" and greatly changed the community at New Lanark. He tore down old buildings and built new ones. He built homes for the workers, had the streets paved, and changed the minimum age at which a child could do factory work from the then established age of six to that of ten years. In making such changes Owen had to fight against two formidable opponents: his partners at the mill and the townspeople themselves. Owen's partners were incensed at the idea that company funds were being used for the welfare of the workers, and often they tried to prevent him from using money for this purpose. As to the townspeople, they were very suspicious of these reforms and considered many of the changes too revolutionary. They were, for example, accustomed to their young children working in the mills in order to supplement the family income, and Owen was changing that.

If there was any one subject that Owen was interested in more than any other, it was education. Throughout his life, he took an interest in the educational systems of many nations and maintained a constant interest in new developments in this field. Owen once offered a thousand pounds to the national schools of Scotland if they would begin to admit children of every creed, and only half that amount if they refused. The school system rejected the first offer, but accepted the five hundred pounds. The offer had achieved such publicity, however, that public pressure forced the schools to reconsider their decision, and later, they were opened to the members of any faith. Owen says, "In following up the subject from that period to the present, my mind has attained the knowledge of the all importance of education in its true meaning, for forming a good character, not merely for the present period, but permanently and universally for the human race."[3]

It would not be true to say that Owen believed in the value of education simply for humanitarian reasons. He felt that education,

[2]Robert Owen, *The Life of Robert Owen* (London: G. Bell and Sons, 1920), pp. 85-86.
[3]Robert Owen, *The Life of Robert Owen* (London: G. Bell and Sons, 1920), p. 117.

besides enobling the masses, would insure the safety and progress of society. He constantly deplored the ignorance of the men who worked in manufacturing, and he believed that through education they would become more efficient and productive workers.

He constantly railed against the education then in vogue. Such education, he believed, was inadvertently designed to make a child disgusted with education. He felt that such education had largely an injurious effect upon those whom it was supposed to elevate. Moreover, he thought that educators did not realize the importance of environment in education. He believed that the great differences in men were due to environment, and that since environment is a factor which is largely under human control, humans can correct environmental conditions so as to create a better race of men. Owen was quite insistent on the point that character was not created "by" the individual, but rather, "for" him, by the type of society in which he lived. He believed that most men had bad characters only because they had been taught principles which were erroneous, and that once correct principles were taught, then mankind would begin to improve.

Character building is the very key to Owen's social and educational doctrines. He not only believed that a child's character could be changed through education, he believed that children collectively could be formed into desirable human characters. Such character training, he believed, could best be achieved when the child was very young.

In education, Owen was the first to set up Infant Schools. He recognized, in connection with this, the importance of play, and also the necessity of teacher-training in order to implant ideas in the children which would be conducive to forming a good character. Although the children were not admitted to formal education until they were five, they received instruction at a public playground from the time they could walk. Owen remarks about the success of this project in his autobiography:

> The parents at first could not understand what I was going to do with their little children at _two_ years of age, but seeing the results produced they became eager to send their infants at one year old, and inquired if I could not take them yet younger. [4]

Owen acquired his educational ideas from many different sources. He even visited Pestalozzi at Yverdun. Owen's comment about the great teacher was that, "His theory was good, but his means and experience were very limited, and his principles were

[4]Robert Owen, _The Life of Robert Owen_ (London: G. Bell and Sons, 1920), p. 186.

those of the old system."[5] However, one may discern the Pestalozzian influence upon many of the educational ideas of Owen. The use of "sense impression" in the form of objects and pictures, the development of "symmetrical" education, and the use of education for the purpose of creating a better society are all principles advocated by the Pestalozzian school and accepted by Owen in his schools at New Lanark. Owen sent his own sons to Hofwyl, which was a Pestalozzian school. Certainly, the Pestalozzian school, no matter what defects Owen found in the master, was more preferable to him than the educational systems of Lancaster and Bell which were then in much use. Lancaster believed that his "monitorial" system was an answer to the "mass" education of the poor. Owen saw this as no kind of education at all, but merely a perpetuation of the erroneous principles of life, which had led to the present state of man's bad character.

Owen realized that you have to create interest as well as instruct, and that you have to create imagination rather than memory. He felt that children should understand what they were learning, as well as enjoy it. He believed that children should be educated without punishment or any fear of punishment, and he attributed the happiness of his pupils in the schools of New Lanark to this principle.

The schools at New Lanark were by no means a fullfillment of Owen's extensive plans for education, and it was his aim that the pupils devote not so much time to subject-matter, as to the development of brotherhood. He hoped that his pupils would carry this idea of brotherhood to all parts of the outside world.

A NEW VIEW OF SOCIETY — Robert Owen*

As a partner of the New Lanark Twist Company, Robert Owen proposes a plan for making the community of New Lanark, Scotland, a well-governed human society based on high ideals, as well as to provide a practical system for the poor and working classes throughout Great Britain. In the following selections, Owen points out some of the educational aims, practices, and principles, inherent to his system.

That which has been hitherto done for the community at New Lanark, as described in the Second Essay, has chiefly consisted in withdrawing some of those circumstances which tended to generate, continue, or increase early bad habits; that is to say, undoing that which society had from ignorance permitted to be done.

[5] *Ibid.*, p. 244.
*Robert Owen, *A New View of Society* (London: J. M. Dent and Sons, Ltd., 1927), pp. 39-42, 47-51. This work was published in London in 1816.

To effect this, however, was a far more difficult task than to train up a child from infancy in the way he should go; for that is the most easy process for the formation of character; while to unlearn and to change long acquired habits is a proceeding directly opposed to the most tenacious feelings of human nature.

Nevertheless, the proper application steadily pursued did effect beneficial changes on these old habits, even beyond the most sanguine expectations of the party by whom the task was undertaken.

The principles were derived from the study of human nature itself, and they could not fail of success.

Still, however, very little, comparatively speaking, had been done for them. They had not been taught the most valuable domestic and social habits: such as the most economical method of preparing food; how to arrange their dwellings with neatness, and to keep them always clean and in order; but, what was of infinitely more importance, they had not been instructed how to train their children to form them into valuable members of the community, or to know that principles existed, which, when properly applied to practice from infancy, would ensure from man to man, without chance of failure, a just, open, sincere, and benevolent conduct.

It was in this stage of the progress of improvement, that it became necessary to form arrangements for surrounding them with circumstances which should gradually prepare the individuals to receive and firmly retain those domestic and social acquirements and habits. For this purpose a building, which may be termed the "New Institution," was erected in the center of the establishment, with an enclosed area before it. The area is intended for a playground for the children of the villagers, from the time they can walk alone until they enter the school.

It must be evident to those who have been in the practice of observing children with attention, that much of good or evil is taught to or acquired by a child at a very early period of its life; that much of temper or disposition is correctly or incorrectly formed before he attains his second year; and that many durable impressions are made at the termination of the first twelve or even six months of his existence. The children, therefore, of the uninstructed and ill-instructed, suffer material injury in the formation of their characters during these and the subsequent years of childhood and of youth.

It was to prevent, or as much as possible to counteract, these primary evils, to which the poor and working classes are exposed when infants, that the area became part of the New Institution.

Into this playground the children are to be received as soon as they can freely walk alone; to be superintended by persons instructed to take charge of them.

As the happiness of man chiefly, if not altogether, depends on his own sentiments and habits, as well as those of the individuals around him; and as any sentiments and habits may be given to all infants, it becomes of primary importance that those alone should be given to them which can contribute to their happiness. Each child, therefore, on his entrance into the playground, is to be told in lanugage he can understand, that "he is never to injure his play-fellows; but that, on the contrary, he is to contribute all in his power to make them happy." This simple precept, when comprehended in all its bearings, and the habits which will arise from its early adoption into practice, if no counteracting principle be forced upon the young mind, will effectually supersede all the errors which have hitherto kept the world in ignorance and misery. So simple a precept, too, will be easily taught, and as easily acquired; for the chief employment of the superintendents will be to prevent any deviation from it in practice. The older children, when they shall have experienced the endless advantages from acting on this principle, will, by their example, soon enforce the practice of it on the young strangers; and the happiness which the little groups will enjoy from this rational conduct, will ensure its speedy and general and willing adoption. The habit also which they will acquire at this early period of life by continually acting on the principle will fix it firmly, and it will become easy and familiar to them, or, as it is often termed, natural.

Thus, by merely attending to the evidence of our senses respecting human nature, and disregarding the wild, inconsistent, and absurd theories in which man has been hitherto trained in all parts of the earth, we shall accomplish with ease and certainty the supposed Herculean labor of forming a rational character in man, and that, too, chiefly before the child commences the ordinary course of education.

The character thus early formed will be as durable as it will be advantageous to the individual and to the community; for by the constitution of our nature, when once the mind fully understands that which is true, the impression of that truth cannot be erased except by mental disease or death; while error must be relinquished at every period of life, whenever it can be made manifest to the mind in which it has been received. This part of the arrangement, therefore, will effect the following purposes:

The child will be removed, so far as is at present practicable, from the erroneous treatment of the yet untrained and untaught parents.

The parents will be relieved from the loss of time and from the care and anxiety which are now occasioned by attendance on their children from the period when thay can go alone to that at which they enter the school.

The child will be placed in a situation of safety, where, with its future school-fellows and companions, it will acquire the best habits and principles, while at meal times and at night it will return to the caresses of its parents; and the affections of each are likely to be increased by the separation.

The area is also to be a place of meeting for the children from five to ten years of age, previous to and after school-hours, and to serve for a drill ground, the object of which will be hereafter explained; and a shade will be formed, under which in stormy weather the children may retire for shelter.

. . . .

The time the children will remain under the discipline of the playground and school will afford all the opportunity that can be desired to create, cultivate, and establish those habits and sentiments which tend to the welfare of the individual and of the community. And in conformity to this plan of proceeding, the precept which was given to the child of two-years old, on coming into the playground, "that he must endeavor to make his companions happy," is to be renewed and enforced on his entrance into the school: and the first duty of the schoolmaster will be to train his pupils to acquire the practice of always acting on this principle. It is a simple rule, the plain and obvious reasons for which children at an early age may be readily taught to comprehend, and as they advance in years, become familiarized with its practice, and experience the beneficial effects to themselves, they will better feel and understand all its important consequences to society.

Such then being the foundation on which the pratical habits of the children are to be formed, we proceed to explain the super-structure.

In addition to the knowledge of the principle and practice of the above-mentioned precept, the boys and girls are to be taught in the school to read well, and to understand what they read; to write expeditiously a good legible hand; and to learn correctly, so that they comprehend and use with facility the fundamental rules of arithmetic. The girls are also to be taught to sew, cut out, and make up useful family garments; and, after acquiring a sufficient knowledge of these, they are to attend in rotation in the public kitchen and eating rooms, to learn to prepare wholesome food in an economical manner, and to keep a house neat and well arranged.

It was said that the children are to be taught to read well, and to understand what they read.

In many schools, the children of the poor and laboring classes are never taught to understand what they read; the time therefore which is occupied in the mockery of instruction is lost. In other schools, the children, through the ignorance of their instructors, are taught to believe without reasoning and thus never to think or to reason correctly. These truly lamentable practices cannot fail to indispose the young mind for plain, simple, and rational instruction.

The books by which it is now the common custom to teach children to read, inform them of anything except that which, at their age, they ought to be taught; hence the inconsistencies and follies of adults. It is full time that this system should be changed. Can man, when possessing the full vigor of his faculties, form a rational judgment on any subject, until he has first collected all the facts respecting it which are known? Has not this been, and will not this ever remain, the only path by which human knowledge can be obtained? Then children ought to be instructed on the same principles. They should first be taught the knowledge of facts, commencing with those which are most familiar to the young mind, and gradually proceeding to the most useful and necessary to be known by the respective individuals in the rank of life in which they are likely to be placed; and in all cases the children should have as clear an explanation of each fact as their minds can comprehend, rendering those explanations more detailed as the child acquires strength and capacity of intellect.

As soon as the young mind shall be duly prepared for such instruction, the master should not allow any opportunity to escape that would enable him to enforce the clear and inseparable connection which exists between the interest and happiness of each individual and the interest and happiness of every other individual. This should be the beginning and end of all instruction; and by degrees it will be so well understood by his pupils that they will receive the same conviction of its truth that those familiar with mathematics now entertain of the demonstrations of Euclid. And when thus comprehended, the all-prevailing principle of known life, the desire of happiness will compel them without deviation to pursue it in practice.

It is much to be regretted that the strength and capacity of the minds of children are yet unknown; their faculties have been hitherto estimated by the folly of the instruction which has been given to them; while, if they were never taught to acquire error, they would speedily exhibit such powers of mind, as would convince the most incredulous how much the human intellect has been injured by the ignorance of former and present treatment.

It is therefore indeed important that the mind from its birth should receive those ideas only which are consistent with each other, which are in unison with all the known facts of the creation, and which are therefore true. Now, however, from the day they are born, the minds of children are impressed with false notions of themselves and of mankind; and in lieu of being conducted into the plain path leading to health and happiness, the utmost pains are taken to compel them to pursue an opposite direction, in which they can attain only inconsistency and error.

Let the plan which has now been recommended be steadily put in practice from infancy, <u>without counteraction from the systems of education which now exist</u>, and characters, even in youth, may be formed, that in true knowledge, and in every good and valuable quality, will not only greatly surpass the wise and learned of the present and preceding times, but will appear, as they really will be, a race of rational or superior beings. It is true, this change cannot be instantaneously established; it cannot be created by magic, or by a miracle; it must be effected gradually — and to accomplish it finally will prove a work of labor and of years. For those who have been misinstructed from infancy, who have now influence and are active in the world, and whose activity is directed by the false notions of their forefathers, will of course endeavor to obstruct the change. Those who have been systematically impressed with early errors, and conscientiously think them to be truths, will of necessity, while such errors remain, endeavor to perpetuate them in their children. Some simple but general method, therefore, becomes necessary to counteract as speedily as possible an evil of so formidable a magnitude.

It was this view of the subject which suggested the utility of preparing the means to admit of evening lectures in the New Institution; and it is intended they should be given, during winter, three nights in the week, alternately with dancing.

To the ill-trained and ill-taught these lectures may be made invaluable; and these are now numerous; for the far greater part of the population of the world has been permitted to pass the proper season for instruction without being trained to be rational; and they have acquired only the ideas and habits which proceed from ignorant association and erroneous instruction.

It is intended that the lectures should be familiar discourses, delivered in plain impressive language, to instruct the adult part of the community in the most useful practical parts of knowledge in which they are deficient, particularly in the proper method of training their children to become rational creatures; how to expend the earnings of their own labor to advantage; and how to appropriate the surplus gains which will be left to them, in order to create a fund which will relieve them from the anxious fear of future want, and thus give them, under the many errors of the present system, that rational confidence in their own exertions and good conduct, without which consistency of character or domestic comfort cannot be obtained, and ought to be expected. The young people may be also questioned relative to their progress in useful knowledge, and allowed to ask for explanations. In short, these lectures may be made to convey, in an amusing and agreeable manner, highly valuable and substantial information to those who are now the most ignorant in the community; and by similar means, which at a trifling expense may be put into action over the whole kingdom, the most important benefits may be given to the laboring classes, and through them, to the whole mass of society.

Chapter Seven

SAMUEL BUTLER
AND *EREWHON*

The word "Erewhon," which represents "Nowhere" (Utopia) roughly spelled backwards, is indicative of Butler's penchant for verbal paradoxes. It is for this reason that *Erewhon* is not an easy book to read and understand. Besides his love of paradox, Butler is also capable of dealing with contradictory viewpoints and expressing them unilaterally, such as in his chapters on "The Book of the Machines," in a manner which almost defies elucidation.

One important point that must be kept in mind while reading this work is that *Erewhon* is not a utopian work in the same sense as is More's *Utopia*, Campanella's *City of the Sun*, or Bellamy's *Looking Backward*. *Erewhon* is not a picture of Butler's Ideal State. It is, rather, a satire against the Victorian Age in which he lived. Most utopian works, and even satirical utopian works, such as *Gulliver's Travels*, can be read as complete stories in themselves, without constant reference to its satiric aspects; but *Erewhon* is almost unintelligible without reference to the kind of world in which Butler lived.

Butler was a profound thinker, a Cambridge graduate, a theologian, a botanist, a painter, and art critic; and he uses the Erewhonians as a foil with which to prick at the foibles of society. He was a true iconoclast, and nothing is sacred from his pen, neither politics, ethics, religion, or education.

Many critics believe that Butler's self-imposed exile to New Zealand for a turn at sheep raising was significant in giving him a fresh look at English society. It was while he was in New Zealand that Darwin's *Origin of Species* appeared, a work which was to have a profound importance on his life. Butler, who had more than a slight knowledge of science to begin with, was ecstatic at first over Darwin's theories on evolution. In June 1863 he wrote an essay to the editor of the Press in New Zealand entitled "Darwin Among the Machines." In this essay he tried to show that machines may someday acquire a definite consciousness and through the evolutionary process, as described by Darwin, come to dominate man himself. Although

Butler often presents outlandish theories as if he were convinced of their truth, yet this treatise may best be taken as a parody on the fact that many men have already become slaves to their machines in the thousands of factories throughout the civilized world. Butler's answer to the possible domination of mankind by machines was expressed in the Erewhonian determination to persist in the systematic destruction of all worldly machinery — a proposal which William Morris *(News from Nowhere)* would have approved.

There is considerable evidence to show that "The Book of the Machines," which comprises chapters twenty-three to twenty-five, and which carries further the ideas expressed in "Darwin Among the Machines," was written prior to the rest of *Erewhon.* It seems quite possible that this writing formed the basis from which the rest of the work evolved.

In *Erewhon,* Butler seems to express two different viewpoints on machines. In one case, there is the fear of machines becoming too powerful and getting the upper hand, and the other view is that machines may serve some useful purpose to man as "extra corporeal limbs." The Erewhonians, however, seem to be inclined to favor the first view.

The Erewhonians, one must remember, are creatures of irony. They are middle-class people, governed entirely by public opinion. They hold disease to be a crime; they follow fashions; they believe only what it is polite to believe; and feel that no one has any right to be young, inexperienced, or ill advised — and in Erewhon, it is appearances, not reality, that really count.

Butler used *Erewhon* as a means for attacking one of his favorite targets, the current method of education. In his account of "The Colleges of Unreason," he satirizes by the name "hypothetics" the custom of the Erewhonians of giving great rewards to the man who can translate good poetry into a hypothetical language. In other words, the less useful a thing was, the more it was valued. The main function of the Professors of Unreason was to take all ideas, render them innocuous, vulgarize them, and then make them popular.

Butler found "hypothetics" in the method and curriculum of the public schools and universities of England. In most schools, he found that learning was being done for "hypothetical" purposes. Pupils were taught subjects merely for the purpose of "mental exercise" and not for the purpose of doing anything with what they had learned. Butler not only foresaw the future abolition of such training, which he called "Academicism," but he also emphasized the importance of Dewey-Kilpatrickian principles of "problem solving" and "learning by doing."

The more I see of academicism the more I distrust it. If I had approached painting as I have approached book-writing and music, that is to say by beginning at once to do what I wanted, or as near as I could to what I could find out of this, and taking pains not by way of solving academic difficulties, in order to provide against practical ones, but by waiting till a difficulty arose in practice and then tackling it, thus making the arising of each difficulty be the occasion for learning what had to be learnt about it – if I had approached painting in this way, I should have been all right. As it is I have been all wrong, and it was South Kensington and Heatherley's that set me wrong. I listened to the nonsense about how I ought to study before beginning to paint, and about never painting without nature, and the result was that I learned to study but not to paint. Now I have got too much to do and am too old to do what I might easily have done, and should have done, if I had found out earlier what writing Life and Habit was the chief thing to teach me.

. . . .

Fortunately for me there are no academies for teaching people how to write books, or I should have fallen into them as I did those for painting and instead of writing should have spent my time and money in being told that I was learning how to write. If I died (I mean, if I had got to die, but might tell students one thing first) I should say: – 'Don't learn to do, but learn in doing. Let your falls not be in a prepared ground, but let them be bona fide falls in the rough and tumble of the world; only, of course, let them be on a small scale in the first instance till you feel your feet safe under you. Act more and rehearse less.'[1]

Butler continues his diatribe against "Academicism" in the twelfth chapter of *Alps and Sanctuaries,* where he says that the most university-and-examination-ridden people in the world are the Chinese, and they are the least progressive. In his *Note-Books* he speaks further in detail about education. On the subject of genius, which is also discussed in *Erewhon,* he writes:

Schools and colleges are not intended to foster genius and to bring it out. Genius is a nuisance, and it is the duty of schools and colleges to abate it by setting genius-traps in its way. They are as the artificial obstructions in a hurdle race – tests of skill and endurance, but in

---

[1]Samuel Butler, *Note-Books of Samuel Butler,* ed. H. F. Jones (New York: M. Kennerley, 1913), pp. 104-105.

themselves useless. Still, so necessary is it that genius and originality should be abated that, did not academies exist, we should have to invent them.[2]

Although Butler wrote a number of works during his lifetime, *Erewhon* and *The Way of All Flesh* remain his best known ones. In writing *Erewhon*, Butler drew heavily upon his experiences in New Zealand. The realistic background of the book, including the traveler's journey to the land of the Erewhonians and his passage over the mountains, correspond greatly to the topography of certain parts of New Zealand.

Erewhon Revisited, the sequel to *Erewhon*, is a much lesser known work. At the conclusion of *Erewhon*, the hero has escaped in a gas-filled balloon. This hero, who is called Mr. Higgs in *Erewhon Revisited*, returns to see what effect his strange departure had on the people. He finds that they considered the event a miracle, and that he has become the deity of a religion called Sunchildism. *Erewhon Revisited* is, according to Paul Elmer More, "Nothing less than an elaborate and vicious satire, in rather bad taste, on the miraculous birth and the Ascension. . . The whole treatise should be regarded as a diatribe against Christian dogma."[3]

Religious dogma in Victorian England was a source of great sorrow for Butler. "Charles-Darwinism," as Butler was prone to call it, also turned out to be a subject of great dissatisfaction. Butler had been an enthusiast of Darwin in the beginning, but later became an opponent of Darwin's evolutionary theories. The great question which Darwin could never answer to Butler's satisfaction was, "Did these changes in Species come about by chance?" The Darwinian theory ascribed the variations to chance, as Butler understood it. The Lamarckian theory, which preceded Darwin by forty years, ascribed the cause of variations to the influence of environment. Butler found the Lamarckian theory much more in line with his own thinking on the subject.

By profession, Butler considered himself foremost a painter, not a writer. In regard to his books, and in particular to *Erewhon*, he says:

> *I never make them: they grow: they come to me and insist on being written, and on being such and such. I did not want to write Erewhon, I wanted to go on painting and found it an abominable nuisance being dragged willy-nilly into writing it. So with all my books – the subjects were never of my own choosing; they pressed*

[2]*Ibid*, p. 180.

[3]Paul Elmer More, "Samuel Butler of Erewhon," *The Unpartizan Review*, 15:39, January-March, 1921.

themselves upon me with more force than I could resist. If I had not liked the subjects I should have kicked, and nothing would have got me to do them at all. As I did like the subjects and the books came and said they were to be written, I grumbled a little and wrote them.[4]

EREWHON - Samuel Butler*

The hero of the story (whose name is disclosed in Erewhon Revisited *as Mr. Higgs) goes to work on a sheep farm in an undisclosed foreign country. When shearing time is over, he obtains permission from his master to start on an expedition over a range of nearby mountains. After several narrow escapes, the young adventurer reaches the top of a pass leading into Erewhon. After being imprisoned by the Erewhonians for three months, he is set free to observe the strange country he has entered. In the following selection, a Mr. Thims (Smith roughly spelled backwards)explains the manner of education practiced in Erewhon.*

After supper Mr. Thims told me a good deal about the system of education which is here practiced. I already knew a part of what I heard, but much was new to me, and I obtained a better idea of the Erewhonian position than I had done hitherto: nevertheless there were parts of the scheme of which I could not comprehend the fitness, although I fully admit that this inability was probably the result of my having been trained so very differently and to my being then much out of sorts.

The main feature in their system is the prominence which they give to a study which I can only translate by the word "hypothetics." They argue thus — that to teach a boy merely the nature of the things which exist in the world around him, and about which he will have to be conversant during his whole life, would be giving him but a narrow and shallow conception of the universe, which it is urged might contain all manner of things which are not now to be found therein. To open his eyes to these possibilities, and so to prepare him for all sorts of emergencies, is the object of this system of hypothetics. To imagine a set of utterly strange and impossible contingencies, and require the youths to give intelligent answers to the questions that arise therefrom, is reckoned the fittest conceivable way of preparing them for the actual conduct of their affairs in after life.

Thus they are taught what is called the hypothetical language for many of their best years — a language which was originally

[4]Samuel Butler, *Note-Books of Samuel Butler,* ed. H. F. Jones (New York: M. Kennerley, 1913), p. 106.

*Samuel Butler, *Erewhon* (New York: E. P. Dutton and Company, 1917), pp. 214-222. This work was originally published in 1872.

composed at a time when the country was in a very different state of civilization to what it is at present, a state which has long since disappeared and been superseded. Many valuable maxims and noble thoughts which were at one time concealed in it have become current in their modern literature, and have been translated over and over again into the language now spoken. Surely then it would seem enough that the study of the original language should be confined to the few whose instincts led them naturally to pursue it.

But the Erewhonians think differently; the store they set by this hypothetical language can hardly be believed; they will even give any one a maintenance for life if he attains a considerable proficiency in the study of it; nay, they will spend years in learning to translate some of their own good poetry into the hypothetical language − to do so with fluency being reckoned a distinguishing mark of a scholar and a gentleman. Heaven forbid that I should be flippant, but it appeared to me to be a wanton waste of good human energy that men should spend years and years in the perfection of so barren an exercise, when their own civilization presented problems by the hundred which cried aloud for solution and would have paid the solver handsomely; but people know their own affairs best. If the youths chose it for themselves I should have wondered less; but they do not choose it; they have it thrust upon them, and for the most part are disinclined towards it. I can only say that all I heard in defense of the system was insufficient to make me think very highly of its advantages.

The arguments in favor of the deliberate development of the unreasoning faculties were more cogent. But here they depart from the principles on which they justify their study of hypothetics; for they base the importance which they assign to hypothetics upon the fact of their being a preparation for the extraordinary, while their study of Unreason rests upon its developing those faculties which are required for the daily conduct of affairs. Hence their professorships of Inconsistency and Evasion, in both of which studies the youths are examined before being allowed to proceed to their degree in hypothetics. The more earnest and conscientious students attain to a proficiency in these subjects which is quite surprising; there is hardly any inconsistency so glaring but they soon learn to defend it, or injunction so clear that they cannot find some pretext for disregarding it.

Life, they urge, would be intolerable if men were to be guided in all they did by reason and reason only. Reason betrays men into the drawing of hard and fast lines, and to the defining by language − language being like the sun, which sears and then scorches. Extremes are alone logical, but they are always absurd; the mean is illogical, but an illogical mean is better than the sheer absurdity of an extreme. There are no follies and no unreasonableness so great as those which can apparently be irrefragably defended by reason itself, and there is hardly an error into which men may not easily be led if they base their conduct upon reason only.

Reason might very possibly abolish the doubly currency; it might even attach the personality of Hope and Justice. Besides, people have such a strong natural bias towards it that they will seek it for themselves and act upon it quite as much as or more than is good for them: there is no need of encouraging reason. With unreason the case is different. She is the natural complement of reason, without whose existence reason itself were non-existent.

If, then, reason would be non-existent were there no such thing as unreason, surely it follows that the more unreason there is, the more reason there must be also? Hence the necessity for the development of unreason, even in the interests of reason herself. The Professors of Unreason deny that they undervalue reason: none can be more convinced than they are, that if the double currency cannot be rigorously deduced as a necessary consequence of human reason, the double currency should cease forthwith; but they say that it must be deduced from no narrow and exclusive view of reason which should deprive that admirable faculty of the one-half of its existence. Unreason is a part of reason; it must therefore be allowed its full share in stating the initial conditions.

Of genius they make no account, for they say that every one is a genius, more or less. No one is so physically sound that no part of him will be even a little unsound, and no one is so diseased but that some part of him will be healthy – so no man is so mentally and morally sound, but that he will be in part both mad and wicked; and no man is so mad and wicked but he will be sensible and honorable in part. In like manner there is no genius who is not also a fool, and no fool who is not also a genius.

When I talked about originality and genius to some gentlemen whom I met at a supper party given by Mr. Thims in my honor, and said that original thought ought to be encouraged, I had to eat my words at once. Their view evidently was that genius was like offenses – needs must that it come, but woe unto that man through whom it comes. A man's business, they hold, is to think as his neighbors do, and Heaven help him if he thinks good what they count bad. And really it is hard to see how the Erewhonian theory differs from our own, for the word "idiot" only means a person who forms his opinions for himself.

The venerable Professor of Wordly Wisdom, a man verging on eighty but still hale, spoke to me very seriously on this subject in consequence of the few words that I had imprudently let fall in defense of genius. He was one of those who carried most weight in the university, and had the reputation of having done more perhaps than any other living man to suppress any kind of originality.

"It is not our business," he said, "to help students to think for themselves. Surely this is the very last thing which one who wishes them well should encourage them to do. Our duty is to ensure that they shall think as we do, or at any rate, as we hold is expedient to say we do." In some respects, however, he was thought to hold somewhat radical opinions, for he was President of the Society for the Suppression of Useless Knowledge, and for the Completer Obliteration of the Past.

As regards the tests that a youth must pass before he can get a degree, I found that they have no class lists, and discourage anything like competition among the students; this, indeed, they regard as self-seeking and unneighborly. The examinations are conducted by way of papers written by the candidate on set subjects, some of which are known to him beforehand, while others are devised with a view of testing his general capacity and savoir faire. My friend the Professor of Wordly Wisdom was the terror of the greater number of students; and, so far as I could judge, he very well might be, for he had taken his Professorship more seriously than any of the other Professors had done. I heard of his having plucked one poor fellow for want of sufficient vagueness in his saving clauses paper. Another was sent down for having written an article on a scientific subject without having made free enough use of the words "carefully," "patiently," and "earnestly." One man was refused a degree for being too often and too seriously in the right, while a few days before I came a whole batch had been plucked for insufficient distrust of printed matter.

About this there was just then rather a ferment, for it seems that the Professor had written an article in the leading university magazine, which was well known to be by him, and which abounded in all sorts of plausible blunders. He then set a paper which afforded the examinees an opportunity of repeating these blunders − which, believing the article to be by their own examiner, they of course did. The Professor plucked every single one of them, but his action was considered to have been not quite handsome.

I told them of Homer's noble line to the effect that a man should strive ever to be foremost and in all things to outvie his peers;

but they said no wonder the countries in which such a detestable maxim was held in admiration were always flying at one another's throats.

"Why," asked one Professor, "should a man want to be better than his neighbors? Let him be thankful if he is no worse."

I ventured feebly to say that I did not see how progress could be made in any art or science, or indeed in anything at all, without more or less self-seeking, and hence unamiability.

"Of course it cannot," said the Professor, "and therefore we object to progress."

Chapter Eight

EDWARD BELLAMY AND *LOOKING BACKWARD*

Bellamy, as Joseph Schiffman points out in the preface to the 1959 edition of *Looking Backward,* is a superb rhetorician, an artful homilist, a skillful user of the Socratic method of argument, and a parodist of uncommon ability. These, and other reasons, help to explain why this utopian work made such a tremendous impression upon the American public when it first appeared in 1888, and why it still holds its popularity even today.

Bellamy's writings evidence literary skill, suggestions for economic and social reconstruction, as well as a philosophical approach toward the problems of man and society. That Bellamy had a very definite "philosophy of life" is shown not only in *Looking Backward* but also in his *The Religion of Solidarity,* published in 1887, which contains philosophical reflections about religion, life, relationships between the sexes, and the concept of genius. Arthur E. Morgan, who is Bellamy's principal biographer, states that he considers Bellamy a philosopher. Not a philosopher in the sense that he had a logical coherent system of thought, but rather in the sense that he was dedicated to the prodding of the state (a nineteenth-century gadfly), and indulged in efforts to establish practical improvements in the social system. As to the manner of his philosophizing, Morgan goes on to say:

> *It is a not uncommon method of the philosopher – though he may not be aware of the fact – first to arrive at his final conclusions by a process of intuition, and then to build an imposing system of reasoning to justify them. Very often the intuitive conclusions are sound, though the processes of reasoning by which, perhaps, he thinks he arrived at them are inconclusive.*[2]

---

[1]Edward Bellamy, *Looking Backward* (New York: Harper and Brothers, 1959), p. xiii. This work was originally published by Houghton, Mifflin Company in 1888.

[2]Arthur E. Morgan, *The Philosophy of Edward Bellamy* (New York: Kings Crown Press. 1945), p. 65.

This was the method that Bellamy used. He admitted that in the writing of *Looking Backward* he was simply putting down ideas about a future society without any conscious realization that they would lead to a movement for social reform. When he saw, however, the impact and the influence these ideas had, he rewrote the book to further stimulate and encourage readers toward the task of building a new society. Bellamy also became involved in a movement called "Nationalism" that was devoted to a propagation of his doctrines, and which he participated in until his death.

In *Looking Backward* many of Bellamy's major reflections on life are presented in one form or another; but the dominant theme is a criticism of nineteenth-century society. He had a moral indictment to preach against the few men who had accumulated great wealth, and who used their wealth in a manner that was detrimental to the public good. It was a time of great trusts like the Standard Oil Company and United States Steel. It was a period of great labor strife in which employer and employee were pitted against each other in wars of the most brutal sort, resulting in one case in the infamous Haymarket riot in Chicago on May 4, 1886, just a short time before the publication of his book. Bellamy believed that the unfair distribution of wealth in this country was the cause of the labor-management controversy, and he pictured a utopia where there would be an equalization of wealth with the nation becoming both the employer and the benefactor of the worker.

When *Looking Backward* first appeared, the charge was immediately made that this work had a strong Marxist bent. Bellamy persistently refuted this view, and though *Das Kapital* was having quite a vogue in America at the time, Bellamy argued that there were more differences than similarities between the two works. He was indeed advocating socialism, but he pointed out that it was to be American socialism, dedicated to the principles embodied in the Constitution and the Declaration of Independence. Bellamy did not accept the Marxist view that class warfare was inevitable and believed that changes could be made in society without revolution. Bellamy also disagreed with Marx that trusts and large businesses were necessarily man's enemies. He pictured a society where trusts and businesses were to become the servants of man rather than his enslavers.

In comparing *Looking Backward* with *Das Kapital* many critics feel that Bellamy's views are more of an emotional appeal for a new society, whereas Marx's approach was by far a more rational criticism of capitalism and the inhumane treatment of the workingman. Bellamy relied upon intuition and a vague acceptance of socialist ideals, whereas the Marxist approach was the more reasoned, logical, and consistent one. Yet Bellamy's ideas about American socialism became very appealing to American visionaries since they did not advocate an overthrow of the existing social system as the Marxist approach did, but merely sought to reform it by bringing the existing system into harmony with humanistic ideas about man and society.

Like Marx, Bellamy believed that the key to a new society lay in a just distribution of wealth and labor, but it was to be a distribution based upon the increased development of technology and the planning of a society where men were unable to hurt and enslave each other. Marx believed that human nature could and should be changed, and that when this happened, the state as a symbol of compulsion and control will have withered away. But in Bellamy's new world in the year 2000 we find that man's nature has not basically changed. It is only that the social institutions of the new society are arranged in such a way that the anti-social attitudes which were encouraged in nineteenth-century society are prevented from operating.

Bellamy is, moreover, a decided optimist. In George Orwell's *1984* and in Aldous Huxley's *Brave New World,* we are given a pessimistic and negative-utopian view of future society. For Bellamy, however, the golden age of humanity lies not with the Periclean Greeks, nor with modern-day man and his reactors and computers, but is always in front of us. He believed also, in the manner of Rousseau, that man has natural goodness, but that this natural goodness is often corrupted by the type of society in which man lives. Bellamy believed that through effort and planning, a society such as he outlined could be established, precluding man from indulging in the evil side of his nature and freeing him to create what he calls "the economy of happiness."

It is little wonder, therefore, that Bellamy produced one of the most popular of all utopian novels. *Looking Backward* encouraged the writing of such books as *Looking Further Forward* by Richard Michaelis and *Young West* by Solomon Schindler and attracted followers from many diverse fields, men such as William Allen White, Walter Rauschenbusch, and Eugene V. Debs. In 1935, Weeks, Dewey, and Beard listed independently the twenty-five most influential books written since 1885. All of them listed *Looking Backward* second, just after *Das Kapital.*[3]

---

[3]Edward Weeks, *This Trade of Writing* (Boston: Little, Brown and Company, 1945), pp. 278-281.

Even though they profess a belief in it for slightly different reasons, both Bellamy and Marx recognize the importance of education to the new society. In the following selection from *Looking Backward* (Chapter 21) we see that Bellamy based his utopia upon a solid foundation of total and universal free education; an education which was to be made available to all persons, without exception or condition, until they reached the age of twenty-one. This would mean that all persons in the new society would attend school until after the completion of a college curriculum, after which time they would enter the national industrial army for a three-year training period. Indeed, the idea of universal higher education is the central educational innovation in the entire work.

It is significant, I think, that Bellamy should point out that in his former life he had only a slight interest in educational affairs, for in the creation of his new society it becomes a most significant part. Bellamy's work is so skillfully planned that the main treatise on education, and the comparison between education in the nineteenth-century and the year 2000, is compacted into a single chapter of some eight pages. However, one might say that like Plato's *Republic* and Marx's *Das Kapital*, the entire work is an educational treatise. Bellamy believed that education was the key to an ideal future society, and that men must be educated anew to control and advance the new society.

The extension of the educational program to include higher education for all persons is a prelude to the importance which Bellamy holds for education as a state duty. The belief that one can serve the state better by being better educated is a very significant part of his thinking; nor does he see any discontinuity in an individual passing from elementary schooling to secondary schooling, to college, to the national industrial army, and from there to either a trade or a profession. The process is not one of ends so much for Bellamy, as it is one of logicality. One does not always serve the state best by being in the industrial army or in a profession. Indeed, at certain ages, he serves best by being in school. Only after the completion of the required schooling can the individual serve effectively in the industrial world.

After completing the period of formal education, *i.e.*, from the lower grades through college, all persons, male or female, would be required to enter the national industrial army (which would be rough schooling in labor) for a three-year training period. Then, on the basis of both training in labor and formal schooling, an individual would be put to decide whether to enter permanently into a trade or a profession. In Bellamy's new society, as in Plato's *Republic,* there would be no snobbery or economic deprivation connected with choosing either a trade or a profession, for each person would be considered to be contributing to society those skills at which he or she was most proficient.

In the following selection on education we have a splendid example of an author choosing to deal with those aspects of a problem he feels qualified to discuss, disregarding those aspects of the problem in which he feels he is lacking. For example, Bellamy does not venture to explain the implementation of a national educational program with regard to regional differences or the training of teachers for the new education, nor does he attempt to say what the curriculum of the schools should be. Bellamy is not, nor does he pretend to be, a professional educationist. But, following the great concern with economics which existed in America at the time of the writing of *Looking Backward,* and which was given special prominence through the writings of Marx, Henry George, Adam Smith, and others, Bellamy does attempt to tell us how we are to pay for this new educational program. He points out that since all large-scale operations are proportionally cheaper than small-scale operations, this principle can be applied to education also, and that an end to the dissipation and extravagance of college education (which he does not spell out exactly) would make higher education as cheap as lower education. The problem of teachers' salaries is also briefly disposed of by the economically-minded Bellamy. As in Plato's *Republic,* there would be no monetary advantage in being in a teaching profession, for since all workers in the state are considered to be contributing to society those skills at which they are most adept, no dictinction is made specifically between brain-labor and manual-labor. Hence, teachers would receive only the same proportional support given to other workers, regardless of occupation.

Like Plato, also, Bellamy believed very strongly in a program of physical education which would influence individuals throughout their lives, and he foresaw an improvement of the species to follow from careful attention given to the physical being of men and women by the educational faculty. Physical education was considered by Bellamy to be a state duty, just as mental education and work was, and the aim of physical education, just as the aim of the other two, was to assist in the development of all of the various capacities of an individual to their highest extent.

There is much for educators to glean from a study of *Looking Backward.* First of all, it gives us a pre-Deweyan picture of nineteenth-century education, which, as Bellamy points out, is devoted to keeping man from manual toil, serving as a springboard to the professions and a life of wealthy leisure. Bellamy not only tells us that we need to adapt education to useful social purposes in both the trades and the professions, but he also gives us, *via* his *deus ex machina,* the utopia, an idea of what we might gain through such a renovation of education. Secondly, Bellamy is most specific on the question of whether to direct the bulk of our educational facilities toward the gifted or the non-gifted in society. Bellamy believed that if there was a choice, then by all means the non-gifted should receive the greatest attention. Such a proposal is still revolutionary in nature, even in these progressive times, and even directed toward the country which has been the most successful in the area of "mass" education. The idea of extending "mass" education to include college training is another seldom considered project even in the most advanced educational circles, but certainly one which deserves further consideration. When one seeks the formative feature of Bellamy's thoughts on education, one comes necessarily to the conclusion that in education, as in other fields, he is devoted to a sincere philosophy of humanism. He says, for example:

> *To educate some to the highest degree, and leave the mass wholly uncultivated, as you did, made the gap between them almost like that between different natural species, which have no means of communication. What could be more inhumane than this consequence of a partial enjoyment of education!*[4]

The primary purpose of education, Bellamy believed, was to make people discontent with economic servitude, poverty, and suffering. Thus, we see the establishment of an educational program based upon the highest humanitarian sentiments. Nor does he advocate his ideas as mere chimeras or idle dreams. Perhaps the most significant feature of *Looking Backward* as a utopian work is its practicality. Indeed, this helps to explain why so many of the ideas which Bellamy advanced in 1888 have come into being, and why still others will undoubtedly be realized in future generations.

LOOKING BACKWARD - Edward Bellamy*

Julian West, a young and wealthy Bostonian, also an insomniac, is in the habit of being mesmerized to sleep by a certain Doctor Pillsbury. On this particular occasion, however, the thirtieth day of May, 1887, a Monday, he

[4]Edward Bellamy, *Looking Backward* (New York: Harper and Brothers, 1959), pp. 213-214.
*Edward Bellamy, *Looking Backward* (New York: The Modern Library, 1951), Chapter 21, pp. 176-182. This work was originally published in 1887.

sleeps exactly one hundred and thirteen years, three months, and eleven days, awakening as still a young man on the tenth day of September in the year 2000. He finds himself in the house of a Doctor Leete, a physician of Boston, who becomes one of his guides to this world of the future. Dr. Leete explains the structure of the new society to him in great detail: the system of commerce, the governmental printing department, the way of shopping, the public laundries; and in Chapter 21, proposes to give him an explanation of their system of education.

It had been suggested by Dr. Leete that we should devote the next morning to an inspection of the schools and colleges of the city, with some attempt on his own part at an explanation of the educational system of the twentieth-century.

"You will see," said he, as we set out after breakfast, "many very important differences between our methods of education and yours, but the main difference is that nowadays all persons equally have those opportunities of higher education which in your day only an infinitesimal portion of the population enjoyed. We should think we had gained nothing worth speaking of in equalizing the physical comfort of men without this educational equality."

"The cost must be very great," I said.

"If it took half the revenue of the nation, nobody would grudge it," replied Dr. Leete, "nor even if it took it all save a bare pittance. But in truth the expense of educating ten thousand youth is not ten nor five times that of educating one thousand. The principle which makes all operations on a large scale proportionally cheaper than on a small scale holds as to education also."

"College education was terribly expensive in my day," said I.

"If I have not been misinformed by our historians," Dr. Leete answered, "it was not college education but college dissipation and extravagance which cost so highly. The actual expense of your colleges appears to have been very low, and would have been far lower if their patronage had been greater. The higher education nowadays is as cheap as the lower, as all grades of teachers, like all other workers, receive the same support. We have simply added to the common school system of compulsory education, in vogue in Massachusetts a hundred years ago, a half dozen higher grades, carrying the youth to the age of twenty-one and giving him what you used to call the education of a gentleman, instead of turning him loose at fourteen or fifteen with no mental equipment beyond reading, writing, and the multiplication table."

"*Setting aside the actual cost of these additional years of education,*" I replied, "*we should not have thought we could afford the loss of time from industrial pursuits. Boys of the poorer classes usually went to work at sixteen or younger, and knew their trade at twenty.*"

"*We should not concede you any gain even in material product by that plan,*" Dr. Leete replied. "*The greater efficiency which education gives to all sorts of labor, except the rudest, makes up in a short period for the time lost in acquiring it.*"

"*We should also have been afraid,*" said I, "*that a high education, while it adapted men to the professions, would set them against manual labor of all sorts.*"

"*That was the effect of high education in your day, I have read,*" replied the Doctor; "*and it was no wonder, for manual labor meant association with a rude, coarse, and ignorant class of people. There is no such class now. It was inevitable that such a feeling should exist then, for the further reason that all men receiving a high education were understood to be destined for the professions or for wealthy leisure, and such an education in one neither rich nor professional was a proof of disappointed aspirations, an evidence of failure, a badge of inferiority rather than superiority. Nowadays, of course, when the highest education is deemed necessary to fit a man merely to live, without any reference to the sort of work he may do, its possession conveys no such implication.*"

"*After all,*" I remarked, "*no amount of education can cure natural dullness or make up for original mental deficiencies. Unless the average natural mental capacity of men is much above its level in my day, a high education must be pretty nearly thrown away on a large element of the population. We used to hold that a certain amount of susceptibility to educational influences is required to make a mind worth cultivating, just as a certain natural fertility in soil is required if it is to repay tilling.*"

"*Ah,*" said Dr. Leete, "*I am glad you used that illustration, for it is just the one I would have chosen to set forth the modern view of education. You say that land so poor that the product will not repay the labor of tilling is not cultivated. Nevertheless, much land that does not begin to repay tilling by its product was cultivated in your day and is in ours. I refer to gardens, parks, lawns, and, in general, to pieces of land so situated that, were they left to grow up to weeds and briars, they would be eyesores and inconveniences to all about. They are therefore tilled, and though their product is little, there is yet no land that, in a wider sense, better repays cultivation. So it is with the men and women with whom we mingle in the relations of*" *society, whose voices are always in our ears, whose behavior in innumerable ways affects our enjoyment — who are, in fact, as much conditions of our lives as the air we breathe, or any of the physical elements on which we depend. If, indeed, we could not afford to educate everybody, we should choose the coarsest and dullest by nature, rather than the brightest, to receive what education we could give. The naturally refined and intellectual can better dispense with aids to culture than those less fortunate in natural endowments.*

"To borrow a phrase which was often used in your day, we should not consider life worth living if we had to be surrounded by a population of ignorant, boorish, coarse, wholly uncultivated men and women, as was the plight of the few educated in your day. Is a man satisfied, merely because he is perfumed himself, to mingle with a malodorous crowd? Could he take more than a very limited satisfaction, even in a palatial apartment, if the windows on all four sides opened into stable yards? And yet just that was the situation of those considered most fortunate as to culture and refinement in your day. I know that the poor and ignorant envied the rich and cultured then; but to us the latter, living as they did, surrounded by squalor and brutishness, seem little better off than the former. The cultured man in your age was like one up to the neck in a nauseous bog solacing himself with a smelling bottle. You see, perhaps, now, how we look at this question of universal high education. No single thing is so important to every man as to have for neighbors intelligent, companionable persons. There is nothing, therefore, which the nation can do for him that will enhance so much his own happiness as to educate his neighbors. When it fails to do so, the value of his own education to him is reduced by half, and many of the tastes he has cultivated are made positive sources of pain.

"To educate some to the highest degree, and leave the mass wholly uncultivated, as you did, made the gap between them almost like that between different natural species, which have no means of communication. What could be more inhuman than this consequence of a partial enjoyment of education! Its universal and equal enjoyment leaves, indeed, the differences between men as to natural endowments as marked as in a state of nature, but the level of the lowest is vastly raised. Brutishness is eliminated. All have some inkling of the humanities, some appreciation of the things of the mind, and an admiration for the still higher culture they have fallen short of. They have become capable of receiving and imparting, in various degrees, but all in some measure, the pleasures and inspirations of a refined social life. The cultured society of the nineteenth-century — what did it consist of but here and there a few

microscopic cases in a vast, unbroken wilderness? The proportion of individuals capable of intellectual sympathies or refined intercourse, to the mass of their contemporaries, used to be so infinitesimal as to be in any broad view of humanity scarcely worth mentioning. One generation of the world today represents a greater volume of intellectual life than any five centuries ever did before.

"There is still another point I should mention in stating the grounds on which nothing less than the universality of the best education could now be tolerated," continued Dr. Leete, "and that is, the interest of the coming generation in having educated parents. To put the matter in a nutshell, there are three main grounds on which our educational system rests: first, the right of every man to the completest education the nation can give him on his own account, as necessary to his enjoyment of himself; second, the right of his fellow-citizens to have him educated, as necessary to their enjoyment of his society; third, the right of the unborn to be guaranteed an intelligent and refined parentage."

I shall not describe in detail what I saw in the schools that day. Having taken but slight interest in educational matters in my former life, I could offer few comparisons of interest. Next to the fact of the universality of the higher as well as the lower education, I was most struck with the prominence given to physical culture, and the fact that proficiency in athletic feats and games as well as in scholarship had a place in the rating of the youth.

"The faculty of education," Dr. Leete explained, "is held to the same responsibility for the bodies as for the minds of its charges. The highest possible physical as well as mental development of every one is the double object of a curriculum which lasts from the age of six to that of twenty-one."

The magnificent health of the young people in the schools impressed me strongly. My previous observations, not only of the notable personal endowments of the family of my host, but of the people I had seen in my walks abroad, had already suggested the idea that there must have been something like a general improvement in the physical standard of the race since my day, and now, as I compared these stalwart young men and fresh vigorous maidens with the young people I had seen in the schools of the nineteenth-century, I was moved to impart my thought to Dr. Leete. He listened with great interest to what I said.

"Your testimony on this point," he declared, "is invaluable. We believe that there has been such an improvement as you speak of, but of course it could only be a matter of theory with us. It is an incident of your unique position that you alone in the world of

today can speak with authority on this point. Your opinion, when you state it publicly, will, I assure you, make a profound sensation. For the rest it would be strange, certainly, if the race did not show an improvement. In your day, riches debauched one class with idleness of mind and body, while poverty sapped the vitality of the masses by overwork, bad food, and pestilent homes. The labor required of children, and the burdens laid on women, enfeebled the very springs of life. Instead of these maleficent circumstances, all now enjoy the most favorable conditions of physical life; the young are carefully nurtured and studiously cared for; the labor which is required of all is limited to the period of greatest bodily vigor, and is never excessive; care for one's self and one's family, anxiety as to livelihood, the strain of a ceaseless battle for life — all these influences, which once did so much to wreck the minds and bodies of men and women, are known no more. Certainly, an improvement of the species ought to follow such a change. In certain specific respects we know, indeed, that the improvement has taken place. Insanity, for instance, which in the nineteenth-century was so terribly common a product of your insane mode of life, has almost disappeared, with its alternative, suicide."

Chapter Nine

WILLIAM MORRIS AND
NEWS FROM NOWHERE

William Morris wrote *News from Nowhere* as a refutation of the utopian world of Bellamy's *Looking Backward*. Morris was saddened to find such a life as Bellamy depicted described as a utopian one. He thus set about the task of correcting Bellamy. Unlike Bellamy, who constructed a complicated world of machinery, Morris eschews mechanization. He foresaw a much simpler kind of life. Morris had visited factory towns and felt that no possible good could ever come from the kinds of production he saw in these places. Like Ruskin, Carlyle, and Dickens, he felt that such production only corrupted men's natures, and thus, in his utopia, he constructed a world in which there was to be only the barest minimum of machinery. The important thing, he thought, was for man to return to hand labor, which would serve the dual purpose of creating art while at the same time satisfying his creative capacities.

Morris was first and last an aesthete. He decried the assembly line which stamped out identical products with little or no regard for artistic design. He was himself a designer and a craftsman, as well as a writer. Morris felt that through his artistic studies he had gleaned joys of which most men are not aware. It was this sincere conviction that encouraged him to give up his own life of aesthetic happiness in order to teach others how they too might attain it. He believed that man had somehow taken the wrong road to happiness, a happiness, and a joy in work which had once been experienced in the past (perhaps in the Middle Ages); and he felt that through instruction and guidance, he could help men to experience this rebirth of artistic happiness in the future.

Morris had a very strong regard for the workers of the Middle Ages who had constructed the great cathedrals. He saw this as the golden age of the craftsman, where each person, working on some small component of the church, did his work with the ultimate regard for beauty and form. He felt that the Industrial Revolution had caught men off guard. Now there was no more concern with beauty and form, but rather, with mere production. Such a change, he believed, was demeaning to both the worker and the finished product.

Morris was no mere visionary in his ideals, however, nor someone just disgruntled with the turn of history. He set himself to the job of attempting to redirect society to the better life, and the vehicle which he chose for this action was socialism. Morris felt that he had thoroughly examined how we live under our present system. It is based first of all, he believed, on a state of perpetual war. By "war" Morris was referring not only to armed conflict, but also to business competition. He was glad that Great Britain had lost its "lion's share" of the world market. The war of commerce, he felt, often leads to a shooting war, because it creates hostility among nations and corruption at home. Socialism, he felt, offered peace and friendship instead of war, and he hoped that the civilized nations would band together to form one great community of workers.

Although he wrote a number of pamphlets and tracts which were socialistic in nature, and even one entitled *Why I Am A Socialist*, yet there was fundamental disagreement from many quarters concerning the type of socialism which Morris espoused. There were communists who considered Morris a disciple of their views, and many distributists did likewise. George Bernard Shaw, who knew Morris personally, says that:

> *Morris, when he had to define himself politically, called himself a Communist. Very often, of course, in discussing Socialism, he had to speak of himself as a Socialist, but he jibbed at it internally, and flatly rebelled against such faction labels as Social-democrat and the like. He knew that the essential term, etymologically, historically, and artistically, was Communist; and it was the only word he was comfortable with.*[1]

R. Page Arnot believes that the great myth about Morris is that he has been canonized by the capitalists as a great poet, and a great craftsman, without any recognition of the fact that he was also a Communist revolutionary. As he describes it:

> *Morris set out in* News from Nowhere *to write a Utopian romance about a Communist Society, about what Marx called the 'higher phase' of Communist society, when the state shall have withered away and the Government of Men given way to the Administration of*

---

[1]George Bernard Shaw, *William Morris, As I Knew Him* (New York: Dodd, Mead and Company, 1936), p. 1.

Things . . .the essence of News from Nowhere is the insistence on the necessity of an armed rising and bitter civil war as the only path to socialism for the working class.[2]

Morris was above all else, an artist. Yet he saw the possible need of a revolution to free men from their machines and to separate the manufacturers from their greed. His *News from Nowhere* envisions life after the revolution. Here is a life which is once again consecrated to art; which for Morris, does not mean just sculpture and painting, but the devotion of the working man to producing something which is an embodiment of his highest ideals and capacities. Morris also pictured a world in which brotherly love reigned supreme. He felt that people would be happy, virtuous, and even beautiful provided they were given work to do which challenged their aesthetic spirits.

In his introduction to the Centenary Edition of Morris's writings, G. D. H. Cole, expresses his belief that Morris's writings have dropped out of fashion because much of his writing was really pictorial — "woven tapestries in words." Our age, unlike the Victorian, he points out, does not want pretty pictures: It is suspicious of them. What it wants, is significance and intellectuality, whereas, most of Morris' work is simply sensuous. He further explains the inclusion of *News from Nowhere* in this collection.

News from Nowhere, of course, chose itself. It is the best known, the most revealing, and the widest in its appeal, of all Morris's writings. As a vision of a coming Socialist society, it is easy enough to pick holes in. Never on earth could human affairs run so smoothly as all that, with so little clanking of the machinery, and with so little machinery to clank. Never could the job of getting the world's work done be reduced to quite that idyllic simplicity, even if men and women did limit their wants to what they really wanted and their quarrels to matters really worth quarreling about. Never could the weather be quite so fine, all the colors quite so bright, all the people quite so healthy, good-looking, and good-humored. Never could life be quite so easygoing, or man or nature quite so kind. . . . Morris knew that. News from Nowhere was neither a prophecy nor a promise, but the expression of a personal preference. Morris was saying, "Here is the sort of society I feel I should like to live in. Now tell me yours."[3]

---

[2]R. Page Arnot, "William Morris versus the Morris Myth," *The Labour Monthly,* 16:181, March, 1934.

[3]William Morris, *William Morris,* Centenary Edition, ed. G.D.H. Cole, (London: The Nonesuch Press, 1948), Introduction, p. xvi.

There is no central government, or any masters in this new society. There are only committees, which tend to such things as school construction and bridge building. The people, as in Well's *Men Like Gods,* govern themselves by friendly common sense and "a habit of acting on the whole for the best." The citizens are simple, tolerant, friendly, and free; and because no reward is given for the work they do, they are perfectly happy. Since there is no economic or social competition, they have never known warfare. There is no discontent of any kind. Nor do they have policemen or prisons. Outbreaks of violence, as in *Erewhon,* are treated as forms of mental illness.

Morris does not lay any great hope for achieving his future society through either Power or Worldly Knowledge. The misuse of power by those about him had hardened his reaction to the compulsion of men even for their own good. This explains why there is no governing class in *News from Nowhere.* As to education, he foresaw the use of it, but in a very restricted sense. It was said of Morris that the only money he ever grudged was the twenty pounds his Oxford degree of Master of Arts had cost him. Thus, in *News from Nowhere,* we find little studying. Since history was so shameful, Morris saw little need for studying it. Geography and languages, he felt, were largely a waste of time unless one intended to travel, in which case a person could pick them up naturally, thus saving the trouble of studying them.

The education which Morris experienced in his lifetime he called "class education." Such education, he felt, failed to make a truly humane and fully developed man. Morris turned his back upon education for citizenship, power, or even knowledge. For him, all education was defective which did not, in a very real sense, help people toward an understanding of art. He felt that every child should be trained in some handicraft or in some fine art. A poor education, he believed, is one which prevents people from understanding art; a good education not only aids men toward understanding art but even helps them to create it.

All strife and discord are not erased from the new world which Morris creates in *News from Nowhere.* There is still left, for example, the interminable battle between the sexes. But there are many real changes. There is no longer any misuse of work. There are no political parties. There is no crime. Nor are there any contracts, bonds, or vows, the taking of which, Morris believed, degraded man.

Throughout the reading of *News from Nowhere,* one is conscious of Morris' deeply felt humanitarian impulses. He wanted a simple life for man; a life which was to be beautiful as well as meaningful, and one in which men could experience honesty between each other. He dreamed of a life in which all men were artists, or aspiring to be so, and living a life deeply devoted to art.

NEWS FROM NOWHERE - William Morris*

The author, who calls himself William Guest, awakens from an epoch of rest to find himself transported to a future age. Richard Hammond and his great-grandfather, as two of his guides in this world of the future, discuss with him the current pattern of education.

The road plunged at once into a beautiful wood spreading out on either side, but obviously much further on the north side, where even the oaks and sweet chestnuts were of a good growth; while the quicker-growing trees (amongst which I thought the planes and sycamores too numerous) were very big and fine-grown.

It was exceedingly pleasant in the dappled shadow, for the day was growing as hot as need be, and the coolness and shade soothed my excited mind into a condition of dreamy pleasure, so that I felt as if I should like to go on forever through that balmy freshness. My companion seemed to share in my feelings, and let the horse go slower and slower as he sat inhaling the green forest scents, chief amongst which was the smell of the trodden bracken near the wayside.

Romantic as this Kensington wood was, however, it was not lonely. We came on many groups both coming and going, or wandering in the edges of the wood. Amongst these were many children from six or eight years old up to sixteen or seventeen. They seemed to me to be especially fine specimens of their race, and were clearly enjoying themselves to the utmost; some of them were hanging about little tents pitched on the greensward, and by some of these fires were burning, with pots hanging over them gypsy fashion. Dick explained to me that there were scattered houses in the forest, and indeed we caught a glimpse of one or two. He said they were mostly quite small, such as used to be called cottages when there were slaves in the land, but they were pleasant enough and fitting for the wood.

"They must be pretty well stocked with children," said I, pointing to the many youngsters about the way.

"Oh," said he, "these children do not all come from the near houses, the woodland houses, but from the countryside generally.

*William Morris, News from Nowhere (London: Reeves and Turner, 1891), pp. 28-33, 69-71.

They often make up parties, and come to play in the woods for weeks together in summer-time, living in tents, as you see. We rather encourage them to it; they learn to do things for themselves, and get to notice the wild creatures; and, you see the less they stew inside houses the better for them. Indeed, I must tell you that many grown people will go to live in the forests through the summer; though they for the most part go to the bigger ones, like Windsor, or the Forest of Dean, or the northern wastes. Apart from the other pleasures in it, it gives them a little rough work, which I am sorry to say is getting somewhat scarce for these last fifty years."

He broke off, and then said, "I tell you all this, because I see that if I talk I must be answering questions, which you are thinking, even if you are not speaking them out; but my kinsman will tell you more about it."

I saw that I was likely to get out of my depth again, and so merely for the sake of tiding over an awkwardness and to say something, I said —

"Well, the youngsters here will be all the fresher for school when the summer gets over and they have to go back again."

"School? he said; "yes, what do you mean by that word? I don't see how it can have anything to do with children. We talk, indeed, of a school of herring, and a school of painting, and in the former sense we might talk of a school of children — but otherwise," said he, laughing, "I must own myself beaten."

Hang it! thought I, I can't open my mouth without digging up some new complexity. I wouldn't try to set my friend right in his etymology; and I thought I had best say nothing about the boy-farms which I had been used to call schools, as I saw pretty clearly that they had disappeared; so I said after a little fumbling, "I was using the word in the sense of a system of education."

"Education?" said he, meditatively, "I know enough Latin to know that the word must come from educere, to lead out; and I have heard it used; but I have never met anybody who could give me a clear explanation of what it means."

You may imagine how my new friends fell in my esteem when I heard this frank avowal; and I said, rather contemptuously, "Well, education means a system of teaching young people."

"Why not old people also?" said he with a twinkle in his eye. "But," he went on, "I can assure you our children learn, whether they go through a 'system of teaching' or not. Why, you will not find one of these children about here, boy or girl, who cannot swim; and every one of them has been used to tumbling about the little forest ponies — there's one of them now! They all of them know how to

cook; the bigger lads can mow; many thatch and do odd jobs at carpentering; or they know how to keep shop. I can tell you they know plenty of things."

"Yes, but their mental education, the teaching of their minds," said I, *kindly translating my phrase.*

"Guest," said he, *"perhaps you have not learned to do these things I have been speaking about; and if that's the case, don't you run away with the idea that it doesn't take some skill to do them, and doesn't give plenty of work for one's mind: you would change your opinion if you saw a Dorsetshire lad thatching, for instance. But, however, I understand you to be speaking of book-learning; and as to that, it is a simple affair. Most children, seeing books lying about, manage to read by the time they are four years old; though I am told it has not always been so. As to writing, we do not encourage them to scrawl too early (though scrawl a little they will), because it gets them into a habit of ugly writing; and what's the use of a lot of ugly writing being done, when rough printing can be done so easily. You understand that handsome writing we like, and many people will write their books out when they make them, or get them written; I mean books of which only a few copies are needed — poems, and such like, you know. However, I am wandering from my lambs; but you must excuse me, for I am interested in this matter of writing, being myself a fair writer."*

"Well," said I, *"about the children; when they know how to read and write, don't they learn something else — languages for instance?"*

"Of course," he said; *"sometimes even before they can read, they can talk French, which is the nearest language talked on the other side of the water; and they soon get to know German also, which is talked by a huge number of communes and colleges on the mainland. These are the principal languages we speak in these islands, along with English or Welsh, or Irish, which is another form of Welsh; and children pick them up very quickly, because their elders all know them; and besides our guests from over the sea often bring their children with them, and the little ones get together, and rub their speech into one another."*

"And the older languages?" said I.

"Oh, yes," said he, *"they mostly learn Latin and Greek along with the modern ones, when they do anything more than merely pick up the latter."*

"And history?" said I, *"how do you teach history?"*

"Well," said he, *"when a person can read, of course he reads what he likes to; and he can easily get someone to tell him what are*

the best books to read on such or such a subject, or to explain what he doesn't understand in the books when he is reading them ."

"Well," said I, "what else do they learn? I suppose they don't all learn history?"

"No, no," said he, "some don't care about it; in fact, I don't think many do. I have heard my great-grandfather say that it is mostly in periods of turmoil and strife and confusion that people care much about history; and you know," said my friend, with an amiable smile, "we are not like that now. No; many people study facts about the make of things and the matters of cause and effect, so that knowledge increases on us, if that be good; and some, as you heard about friend Bob yonder, will spend time over mathematics. 'Tis no use forcing people's tastes."

Said I: "But you don't mean that children learn all these things?"

Said he: "That depends on what you mean by children; and also you must remember how much they differ. As a rule, they don't do much reading, except for a few story books, till they are about fifteen years old; we don't encourage early bookishness: though you will find some children who will take to books very early; which perhaps is not good for them; but it's no use thwarting them; and very often it doesn't last long with them, and they find their level before they are twenty years old. You see, children are mostly given to imitating their elders, and when they see most people about them engaged in genuinely amusing work, like house-building and street-paving, and gardening, and the like, that is what they want to be doing; so I don't think we need fear having too many book-learned men."

What could I say? I sat and held my peace, for fear of fresh entanglements. Besides, I was using my eyes with all my might, wondering as the old horse jogged on, when I should come into London proper, and what it would be like now.

But my companion couldn't let his subject quite drop, and went on meditatively:

"After all, I don't know that it does them much harm, even if they do grow up book-students. Such people as that, 'tis a great pleasure seeing them so happy over work which is not much sought for. And besides, these students are generally such pleasant people; so kind and sweet tempered; so humble, and at the same time so anxious to teach everybody all that they know. Really, I like those that I have met prodigiously."

Said I: "I want an extra word or two about your ideas of education; although I gathered from Dick that you let your children run wild and didn't teach them anything; and in short, that you have so refined your education, that now you have none."

"Then you gathered left-handed," quoth he. "But of course I understand your point of view about education, which is that of times past, when 'the struggle for a slave's rations on one side, and for a bouncing share of the slaveholders' privilege on the other,' pinched 'education' for most people into a niggardly dole of not very accurate information; something to be swallowed by the beginner in the art of living whether he liked it or not, and was hungry for it or not: and which had been chewed and digested over and over again by people who didn't care about it in order to serve it out to other people who didn't care about it."

I stopped the old man's rising wrath by a laugh, and said: "Well, you were not taught that way, at any rate, so you may let your anger run off you a little."

"True, true," said he smiling. "I thank you for correcting my ill-temper: I always fancy myself as living in any period of which we may be speaking. But, however, to put it in a cooler way: you expected to see children thrust into schools when they had reached an age conventionally supposed to be the due age, whatever their varying faculties and dispositions might be, and when there, with like disregard to facts to be subjected to a certain conventional course of 'learning.' My friend, can't you see that such a proceeding means ignoring the facts of growth, bodily and mental? No one could come out of such a mill uninjured; and those only would avoid being crushed by it who would have the spirit of rebellion strong in them. Fortunately most children have had that at all times, or I do not know that we should ever have reached our present position. Now you see what it all comes to. In the old times all this was the result of poverty. In the nineteenth-century, society was so miserably poor, owing to the systematised robbery on which it was founded, that real education was impossible for anybody. The whole theory of their so-called education was that it was necessary to shove a little information into a child, even if it were by means of torture, and accompanied by twaddle which it was well known was of no use, or else he would lack information lifelong: the hurry of poverty forbade anything else. All that is past; we are no longer hurried, and the information lies ready to each one's hand when his own inclinations impel him to seek it. In this as in other matters we have become wealthy: we can afford to give ourselves time to grow."

"Yes," said I, "but suppose the child, youth, man, never wants the information, never grows in the direction you might hope him to do: suppose, for instance, he objects to learning arithmetic or mathematics; you can't force him when he is grown; can't you force him while he is growing, and oughtn't you to do so?"

"Well," said he, "were you forced to learn arithmetic and mathematics?"

"A little," said I.

"And how old are you now?"

"Say fifty-six," said I.

"And how much arithmetic and mathematics do you know now?" quoth the old man, smiling rather mockingly.

Said I: "None whatever, I am sorry to say."

Hammond laughed quietly, but made no other comment on my admission, and I dropped the subject of education, perceiving him to be hopeless on that side.

Chapter Ten

RALPH ADAMS CRAM AND WALLED TOWNS

Ralph Adams Cram and William Morris had three definite things in common: (1) a hatred of modern life, (2) a love of art, and (3) a belief that the European Middle Ages was the noblest period of man's existence on earth. The fact that *Walled Towns* advocated a desire to return to the kind of monastic existence which was practiced by so many during the Middle Ages does not detract from this as a utopian work, for this is the kind of life Cram envisions for men to return to in the future: a life which would restore to man the great love of art which was so prevalent during the Middle Ages. It was also intended as a work which would show men that there were more suitable governments for life and work than those found in contemporary society.

Cram had many objections to the form of democracy he found in America in the early twentieth-century. He believed that such democracy was not true democracy at all. He felt that there was not true democracy in America just because everyone had an opportunity to participate in electing leaders, formulating policies, and so on. Such opportunities, he felt, merely enabled men, due to their "mass" stupidity, to assist in the appointment of rulers and laws which would deprive them of further freedoms and advantages in life. True democracy, he believed, is one in which wise and just rulers are in control, who will see to it that all men obtain the highest possible freedom and justice, even despite their frequent insistence on being enslaved.

Cram had little regard for "man in the mass," and he believed that this type of man, which was the most common form of human being in the world, had not changed perceptibly in the last six-thousand years. He thought that most men were of the Neolithic type. How could such men accept the responsibility of choosing leaders and participating in government? Only the minority (as Plato pointed out) and not the majority have intelligence and high moral character, and therefore the minority must lead, and the majority must follow. In modern democracy, Cram found just the opposite pattern existing.

He points out in *Convictions and Controversies*[1] that truth and beauty may not be synonymous, but that in a very real sense, beauty is the test of truth. Cram felt that no ugly thing could be valid, whether it be cubist sculpture, Calvinistic theology, go-getter policies, or democratic government. Democratic government is ugly, he feels, because it is in the wrong shape, and he states that no amount of propaganda can convince him that it is other than it is. Cram believed that a study of history shows that we judge past cultures on the basis of their art and reverence for beauty. How then, he asks, will our culture stand up to the same test?

Obviously, Cram felt that we could not pass the test for beauty, and that it was the emergence of mechano-industrialism and politico-social democracy that were largely responsible. The American Revolution, he believed, as well as the French Revolution, were responsible for putting this idea of democracy into men's heads. The tyranny of the kings was bad enough, but in its place, we have substituted the tyranny of the mob and raised the status of the mediocre man. Concomitant with this, grew industrialism. Now the mediocre or Neolithic man could accumulate great wealth and begin to take an even greater interest in politics. Not only did such men become the "captains of industry," but the "captains of nations" as well. These were the same men, Cram points out, who had been so brutalized by the evil conditions existing since the Renaissance that they had lost all feeling for beauty and all sense of justice. Such men, he believes, are now in command of our very way of life. It cannot last, however, and Cram forsees the breakdown of democracy occurring everywhere. The Neolithic man, though thrust into power by circumstances beyond his control, has neither the intelligence nor the leadership to maintain that power. There is a New Medievalism on the rise, Cram believes, in which governments once again will be placed into the hands of the capable few.

Although education cannot be held responsible for man's plight today, since the causes go much deeper, yet it can be accused of assisting in the perpetuation of those presently in power. It is for this reason Cram feels, that it would be unwise for us to put a great deal of faith in education as a means for overcoming our present dilemma.

The primary responsibility of education, Cram believes, is to create great leaders. He wants the schools to develop the kind of men and women who can direct the sort of programs he outlines in *Walled Towns*. The educational reforms which he makes in this work are

---

[1]Ralph Adams Cram, "Challengers of Democracy," *Convictions and Controversies* (Boston: Marshall Jones Company, 1935), p. 117.

part and parcel of his social reforms as a whole, and in regard to higher education for the mediocre or Neolithic man, he says:

> Our educational system should, so far as it is free and compulsory, normally end with the high school grade. Free college, university and technical training should not be provided, except for those who had given unmistakable evidence that they could, and probably would, use it to advantage.[2]

Cram's idea of a college, which he goes into further in *Walled Towns*, is a place with self-contained groups of not more than one hundred and fifty students, segregated in their own residential quad, with a common-room, refectory, and chapel. There are to be a certain number of faculty members in residence, all under one "Head." He suggests that the student body could be gradually increased to accommodate as many as that of a western state university, but states that our present college system of five or ten thousand students, all jostling together in one inchoate mass, eating in mobs, and taking refuge from mere numbers in clubs, fraternities, and secret societies, is so abhorrent that it should be done away with at once.

Like so many other utopianists, Robert Owen in particular, Cram felt that there was a great deal wrong with the education he experienced as a child, and also with the kind of education young people are still experiencing. The primary error in this kind of education, both Owen and Cram believed, was the concentration given to the learning of academic studies, rather than in putting primary concern on the building of character. He says that:

> Education can do much, but what it does, or can do, is to foster and develop <u>inherent possibilities</u>, whether these are of character, intelligence or aptitude: it cannot put into a boy or man what was not there, in <u>posse</u>, at birth, and humanly speaking, the diversity of potential in any thousand units is limited only by the number itself. Whether our present educational methods are those best calculated to foster and develop these inherent possibilities, so varied in nature and degree, is the question, and it is a question the answer to which depends largely on whether we look on intelligence, capacity or character as the thing of greatest moment. For those who believe that character is the thing of paramount importance – amongst whom I count myself – the answer must be in the negative.

. . . .

[2]Ralph Adams Cram, "The Function of Education and Art," *Towards the Great Peace* (Boston: Marshall Jones Company, 1922), p. 163.

...what precisely is the function of formal education. For my own part I can answer this in a sentence. It is primarily the fostering and development of the character-potential inherent in each individual. In this process, intellectual training and expansion and the furthering of natural aptitudes have a part, but this is secondary to the major object which is the development of character.

. . . .

The avowed object of formal education is mental and vocational training, and by no stretch of the imagination can we hold these to be synonymous with character.[3]

Cram believed that in the building of character the emotions play an important part. The schools are charged with the responsibility of properly influencing man's emotional nature; and the emotions are "judiciously stimulated" best through the use of art and religion. The emotions are not to be controlled by the intellect, but the intellect does serve a valuable purpose in balancing these emotions properly. Besides art and religion, Cram believed that the emotional side of students should also be stimulated through the use of competitive athletics, and it was for this reason that he considered athletics to be a very important factor in public education.

In the Middle Ages art and religion were the focal points of society. So too, now, Cram felt, we must reinstate these two great forces in life in order to give meaning to man's existence. Cram saw the building of character to rest predominantly on the bringing of art and religion into the classroom. However, he points out specifically that he does not mean the art and religion of the twentieth-century. Today, art and religion, as well as philosophy, have been corrupted by capitalistic democracy. The art, religion, and philosophy he is referring to belong to the medieval period; but he hopes that man may experience a rebirth of all these things again in the future.

WALLED TOWNS - Ralph Adams Cram*

The author states that he is establishing "a way out," based on the assumption that "modern civilization" is an inferior product, and that democracy, as we know it, is a menace to righteous society. He suggests a communal life based on the precedents of monastic methods within experimental Walled Towns.

[3]Ralph Adams Cram, "The Function of Education and Art," *Towards the Great Peace* (Boston: Marshall Jones Company, 1922), pp. 159-160, 163, 166.

*Ralph Adams Cram, *Walled Towns* (Boston: Marshall Jones Company, 1919), pp. 83-88.

Within the Walled Towns the educational system shows few points of resemblance to the standards and methods still pursued outside. It is universally recognized that the prime object of all education is the development of inherent character, and for this reason it is never divorced from religion; the idea of a rigidly secularized education is abhorrent, and the dwellers in the Walled Towns rightly attribute to its prevalence in the nineteenth-century much of the retrogression in character, the loss of sound standards of value, and the disappearance of leadership which synchronized with the twentieth-century break-down of civilization even if it were not indeed its primary cause. Neither is there any false estimate of the possibilities of education; it is held that while it can measurably develop qualities latent in the child by reason of its racial impulse, it cannot put in what is not there already. The old superstition that education and environment are omnipotent, and that they were the safeguards as well as the justification of democracy, since given an identical environment and equal educational opportunities a hundred children of as many classes, races and antecedents would turn out equal as potential members of a free society, has long since been abandoned. It is impossible to enter into this question at length, but the chief points are these.

Education is not compulsory, but parents are bound to see that their children can "read, write and cipher." Primary schools are maintained by the town and are conducted largely along the lines first developed by Dr. Thomas Edward Shields [prominent Catholic educator] in the early twentieth-century. Beyond primary grades the schools are maintained by various units such as the guilds, the parish and the monasteries and convents. While considerable variation exists as between one school and another, they are all under the supervision of the Director of Education in order that certain standards may be maintained. Variety both in subjects taught and in methods followed is held to be most desirable, and complete freedom of choice exists between the schools, though a parent wishing to send a child to some school other than those maintained by his own guild pays an annual fee for the privilege. Beyond reading, writing, arithmetic and music, which are common to all, the curriculum varies widely, though history, literature and Latin are practically universal. In some schools mathematics will be carried further than in others, in some natural science, while elsewhere literature, history and modern languages will be emphasized. There is no effort to subject all children to the same methods and to force them to follow the same courses, — quite the reverse; neither is the object the carrying of all children through the same schools to the same point. It is held that beyond a certain stage most children profit little or nothing by continued intensive study. On the other hand, there are always those whose desires and capacities would carry them to the limit. These are watched for with the most jealous care, and if a boy or girl shows special aptitude along any particular line he becomes an honor student, and there- after he is in a sense a ward of the community, being sent without charge to the higher schools, the college, and even on occasion to some university beyond the limits of the Walled Town if he can gain there something not available within the walls. Of course any student may continue as far as he likes, or is able, but this is not encouraged except in the case of the honor student, and he must himself meet his own expenses. The authorities are particularly careful to discover any special ability in any of the arts, literature and philosophy, and it is the boast of the Walled Towns that no one who gives promise along any one of these lines need fail of achievement through lack of opportunity. In the case of the various crafts also the same care is exercised, and a boy showing particular aptitude is at once given the opportunity of entrance into the proper guild as an apprentice, after he has been prepared for this by a modified course of instruction adapted to his particular ability.

The college has something the effect of a blending of New College, Oxford, and St. John's, Cambridge. It is perhaps the most beautiful element in the Walled Town, and here every intellectual, spiritual and artistic quality is fostered to the fullest degree. The college is a corporation under control of the alumni and the faculty, not in the hands of trustees, as was the unfortunate fashion amongst American universities in the nineteenth-century. There are many fellowships granted for notable achievements along many lines, and a Fellow may claim free food and lodgings for life, if he choose, the return being certain service of a limited nature in the line of instruction, either as lecturer or preceptor. A few students are received from without the walls, but the number may not exceed five percent of the student body, and high fees are charged for the privilege. There are no regular courses divided into four years. An honor student must take his Bachelor's Degree within six years, his Master's Degree in not less than two years thereafter, and his Doctorate in another four years, otherwise his privilege lapses and he must pay as other students, in which case there are no limits whatever and a man may spend a lifetime in study if he desires – and pay the price. All the regular members of the Faculty must be burgesses, but many lecture courses are given by visiting professors from all parts of the world. Latin is a prerequisite for the Bachelor's and Master's Degrees, and Greek for a Doctorate, whatever the line that may be followed.

As has been said above, the recreation quarter of the town is around a square or garden a short distance from the central square. Here are to be found the public baths and gymnasium, together with a number of gay and attractive cafes and restaurants, the theaters, concert halls, etc. To a very great extent all the music and drama are the product of the people themselves. As has been said, music is almost the foundation of the educational system, therefore trained as they are from earliest childhood, good music, vocal, instrumental, orchestral, even operatic, is a natural and even inevitable result. The same is true of the drama, and nightly plays, operas, concerts are given by the townspeople themselves which reach a standard comparable with that of professionals elsewhere. Now and then, as a mark of special commendation, actors, singers and musicians are invited by the Provost and Council to visit the town, but as a general thing all is done by the people themselves. The moving picture show is prohibited.

Chapter Eleven

H. G. WELLS AND MEN LIKE GODS

H. G. Wells was a writer who was intoxicated with the future. He believed that there were two divergent attitudes toward this subject: first, there is the person who seldom thinks of the future at all, and if so, regards it as a sort of blank nonexistence upon which the advancing present will write events; and the other type is the man who thinks consistently and by preference of the things to come. Wells further believed that the person who related the present only to the past had a legal or submissive type of mind, which was only concerned with the established order, and thus constantly seeking to suppress new trends; whereas the future-oriented man, who was the legislative and creative type of person, was constantly engaged in attacking the *status quo,* and thus altering the established order of things. Wells was decidedly of this latter category. Of all his massive writing, at least one-fourth deals with the future, and he often defended what might be called "a philosophy of futurism" before many learned societies and throughout a battery of writings.

Wells had the notion that man could look at the future scientifically. He not only believed that men could do this but that man does it, and that this is a desirable thing.

> *All applied mathematics resolves into computation to foretell things which otherwise can only be determined by trial. Even in so unscientific a science as economics there have been forecasts. And if I am right in saying that science aims at prophecy, and if the specialist in each science is in fact doing his best now to prophecy within the limits of his field, what is there to stand in the way of our building up this growing body of forecast into an ordered picture of the future that will be just as certain, just as strictly science, and perhaps just as detailed as the picture that has been built up within the last hundred years of the geological past?* [1]

[1] H. G. Wells, *The Discovery of the Future* (London: Jonathan Cape, Ltd., 1913), pp. 35-36.

Wells attempted to look into the future on many occasions. What he saw in the immediate future disturbed him no small bit. The First World War had left an indelible imprint on his mind of useless bloodshed and horror; and the unchangeableness of man's thirst for war and hatred which he saw in contemporary civilization led him to make dire predictions regarding the possibility of a second great war, a war which eventually erupted in the form of World War Two.

Wells saw only one great hope for mankind, and that was to unite politically into a great world state. He believed that a state which was politically united with other states would be permanently at peace. When he first thought of the idea of a world state, he called it "The Utopia of a World State," but he later changed it to "The Project of a World State," for he felt that this was a plan not to be projected into the future, but one which needed to be implemented immediately in order to avoid imminent disaster. He also incorporated into this plan Comenius' idea of creating a common Book of Necessary Knowledge, "which should form the basis and framework for the thoughts and savage imaginations of every citizen in the world."[2] Wells proposed to call such a book "The Bible of Civilization," since it was to be patterned after the Judaic-Christian Bible. Wells was convinced, however, that the old Bible had become separated from the problems of modern man. "It has lost hold," he says, "but nothing has arisen to take its place."[3] Wells suggested that his *The Outline of History* be taken as a sketch of the kind of Bible he meant.

The plea for a "Bible of Civilization," containing above all the tremendous advances made in science, points to Wells' great concern with knowledge and with its dissemination through education. He was often disheartened by the superstitious nonsense and the ill-founded opinions he heard daily about him, coming from people who he believed lived in "An Age of Confusion." He was also realistic enough to know that the schools were doing very little to combat this confusion.

It is the crowning absurdity in the world today that those institutions should go through a solemn parade of preparing the new generation for life and that then, afterwards, a minority of their victims, finding this preparation has left them almost totally unpre-

---

[2]H. G. Wells, *The Salvaging of Civilization* (New York: The Macmillan Company, 1921), p. 97.
[3]H. G. Wells, *The Salvaging of Civilization* (New York: The Macmillan Company, 1921), p. 103.

pared, should have of their own accord to struggle out of our world heap of starved and distorted minds to some sort of a real education.[4]

One reason why education is of primary significance for Wells is because he foresaw the utter impossibility of forming a world state to prevent war so long as men remained uneducated. He realized that it could be education, and only education, which could change man from the essentially self-seeking creature that he is into a being capable of living in harmony with other human beings. In *Men Like Gods,* we are shown what could be, if men were willing to make education their government, so that they could learn and thus begin to exercise their potentialities for human cooperation.

In *Men Like Gods,* Mr. Barnstaple is taken into this world of godlike men by an ingenious yet unchecked experiment performed by two young scientists in this world of the future named Arden and Greenlake. These two were conducting a chemical experiment to see if they could rotate a part of their world into the fourth dimension.

It was at this precise moment that Barnstaple, the London journalist, was traveling in his automobile down Oxford Road toward Windsor. He tells of a few cars passing him and then turning around a bend in the road. When he turns around this same bend, he sees nothing but a long stretch of roadway, and the cars which just passed him have disappeared. He hears a funny snapping sound, has a moment of unconsciousness, and then is whisked into Arden and Greenlake's experiment, finding himself suddenly transported to a strange new country.

There is a regulated climate here, as well as regulated cleanliness and learning. The population is kept at one-fifth that of earth's, and the people are so healthy that a man of ninety looks like a man of forty. The mentality of the people is such that an adolescent boy (like Crystal, one of Mr. Barnstaple's guides) has an intelligence equal to that of a mature earthling.

Things are regulated in *Men Like Gods,* but not by law. Nor is there any power through law to enforce the regulations. A sort of collective wisdom abounds, so that people always tend to do the right thing. Whenever anyone refuses to observe a certain regulation, an inquiry is made into his mental health.

Almost like a preface to *Men Like Gods,* which was written in 1923, is *A Modern Utopia,* which precedes it by eighteen years. In *A*

---

[4]H. G. Wells, *What Are We Going to Do with Our Lives* (New York: Doubleday, Doran, and Company, 1931), p. 20.

Modern Utopia, unlike *Men Like Gods,* there are still some troubles in utopia. There is friction, waste, and laziness. There is also a ruling class of aristocrats, like Plato's Guardians, who are known as the Samurai. These do all of the doctoring, judging, voting and teaching. It is what Wells calls a "voluntary nobility," and anyone can become a Samurai provided he is able to pass certain tests and agrees to live according to the Rule. The Samurai are not allowed to indulge in tobacco, alcoholic drinks, or drugs, nor can they engage in commerce, which is considered degrading. Each active Samurai is also required to spend at least one week per year in solitude and under primitive conditions. This is designed for the purpose of meditation, as well as to assist in the development of self-reliance and endurance.

In *Men Like Gods,* all men have become Samurai, or are in the process of becoming so. This world is five centuries ahead of ours in time, and all of the confusion and friction which so characterize our world, and which is only partially mitigated in *A Modern Utopia,* have completely disappeared.

In *Men Like Gods,* Wells tells how great the struggles of the educationists were against the class of "irresponsible rich people," against "greedy, passionate, prejudiced and self-seeking men," and how the battle went on for five centuries, causing the death of over a million martyrs. It was only when the educationists won, and were able to exercise power through the schools and colleges, that the new order began to emerge. It is in this fantasy, also, that Wells implies that in each man there is some seed of greatness — just waiting for the food which will activate it. The food is, of course, education. Thus, with this "Food of the Gods," a gigantic race of supermen is formed, who bring a nobler order of things into being.

This work serves to point out Wells' bitterness with contemporary education in England. He felt that a reform was greatly overdue, a reform which would deal with the community as a whole. His proposal was to reorganize the schools along the lines of big production by utilizing modern appliances, economizing teaching energy, and centralizing its control. As a former schoolteacher, he propounds his points from firsthand experience. In a variety of writings, Wells lashes out at English education, from elementary instruction to higher education.

In *Mankind in the Making,* he speaks about this constant prodding of education, and educators, and the entertainment it affords him:

> *Scolding the schoolmaster, gibing at the schoolmaster, guying, afflicting and exasperating the schoolmaster in every conceivable*

*way, is an amusement so congenial to my temperament that I do not
for one moment propose to abandon it.*[5]

One of the important ethical problems of education in *Men
Like Gods,* as Doughty[6] points out, is the conflict between two
traditional and seemingly contradictory views of education. There is
one general view of education seen as an entity apart from other
factors and controls; and another view wherein education is seen as a
process of regimentation in the interests of the stabilized social
order. Wells combines educational progress and individuality with
political and social stability, a feat not attempted in any previous
utopian work.

If there was any one thing that Wells believed in unreservedly, it
was progress. In his writings, he constantly encourages his readers to
work more and to learn more in order to hasten the dawn of the new
day, when man shall have become free of war, ignorance, and slavery.
The alternative to progress, he believes, is disaster. This effort to
avoid disaster, he felt, was "a race between education and catastrophe," and to fail could mean the loss of civilization. Mr. Wells, many
believe, has prophesied well the emerging twentieth-century dilemma
which now faces us.

War was always the thing he hated most. His primary aim in life
was to try and teach m en to live in peace with each other. When he
died in 1946, the world had just gone through another great and
bloody war. One of the tributes paid to Wells after his death points
to his humanistic spirit and his undying efforts to educate his
fellowmen to peace.

> *Wells lived on the future as some men do on the past. The future was
> the schoolmaster's rod with which he threatened us; it was the
> schoolmaster's pointer with which he showed us the way of reason.
> Frank Moore Colby once said of him: 'He is annoyed by the
> senseless refusal of almost everybody to shape his life in such a
> manner as will redound to the advantage of the beings who will
> people the earth a hundred thousand years hence.' This is true; and
> yet there is something to be said for Wells' future-mindedness.
> Perhaps, unless we can learn to think of ourselves as we might be a
> hundred thousand years hence, we shall destroy each other a
> hundred months hence. Perhaps only the Utopians can help us to
> survive. In any case it is clear that the 'practical' men – the generals,*

[5] H. G. Wells, *Mankind in the Making* (New York: Charles Scribner's Sons, 1918), p.
209.

[6] F. H. Doughty, *H. G. Wells; Educationist?* (New York: George H. Doran Company,
1927), p. 108ff.

the admirals, the politicians, the dictators, and the owners of great mind-killing magazines — cannot. In the light of The Dark Century to come, Wells' Utopian thought begins to look less fantastic than it did when first we encountered it. He has been right about so many things. Perhaps he was right, too, in his conviction that we would not endure as civilized men unless we educated ourselves, at whatever the cost, into an awareness of our essential unity.[7]

MEN LIKE GODS - H. G. Wells*

Mr. Barnstaple was advised by his doctor to take a holiday in order to relieve neurasthenia caused by his position as junior editor of a newspaper called the Liberal. While driving into the country, the roadway suddenly changes, and Mr. Barnstaple and some other companions whom he met along the way are suddenly whirled into a strange utopian country. During one of his tours of this strange land Mr. Barnstaple meets one of the young boys, named Crystal, who discusses some of the aspects of education in this place.

———————

Presently he found a companion for his rambles, a boy of thirteen, a cousin of Lychnis, named Crystal. He was a curly-headed youngster, brown-eyed as she was; and he was reading history in a holiday stage of his education.

So far as Mr. Barnstaple could gather, the more serious part of his intellectual training was in mathematical work interrelated to physical and chemical science, but all that was beyond an Earthling's range of ideas. Much of this work seemed to be done in cooperation with other boys, and to be what we should call research on earth. Nor could Mr. Barnstaple master the nature of some other sort of study which seemed to turn upon refinements of expression. But the history brought them together. The boy was just learning about the growth of the Utopian social system out of the efforts and experiences of the Ages of Confusion. His imagination was alive with the tragic struggles upon which the present order of Utopia was founded he had a hundred questions for Mr. Barnstaple, and he was full of explicit information which was destined presently to sink down and become part of the foundations of his adult mind. Mr. Barnstaple was as good as a book to him, and he was as good as a guide to Mr. Barnstaple. They went about together talking upon a footing of the completest equality, this rather exceptionally intelli-

[7]Clifton Fadiman, "The Passing of a Prophet," *The Saturday Review of Literature*, 29:4, August 31, 1946.

*H. G. Wells, *Men Like Gods* (New York: The Macmillan Company, 1923), pp. 263-268, 268-270, 272-276.

gent Earthling and this Utopian stripling, who topped him by
perhaps an inch when they stood side by side.

The boy had the broad facts of Utopian history at his fingers'
ends. He could explain and find an interest in explaining how
artificial and upheld the peace and beauty of Utopia still were.
Utopians were in essence, he said, very much what their ancestors
had been in the beginnings of the newer stone age, fifteen-thousand
or twenty-thousand years ago. They were still very much what
Earthlings had been only 600 or 700 generations ago with no time
for any very fundamental changes in the race. There had not been
even a general admixture of races. On Utopia as on earth there had
been dusky and brown peoples, and they remained distinct. The
various races mingled socially but did not interbreed very much;
rather they purified and intensified their racial gifts and beauties.
There was often very passionate love between people of contrasted
race, but rarely did such love come to procreation. There had been a
certain deliberate elimination of ugly, malignant, narrow, stupid and
gloomy types during the past dozen centuries or so; but except for
the fuller realization of his latent possibilities, the common man in
Utopia was very little different from the ordinary energetic and able
people of a later stone-age or early bronze-age community. They
were infinitely better nourished, trained and educated, and mentally
and physically their condition was clean and fit, but they were the
same flesh and nature as we are.

"But," said Mr. Barnstaple, and struggled with that idea for a
time. "Do you mean to tell me that half the babies born on earth
today might grow to be such gods as these people I meet?"

"Given our air, given our atmosphere."

"Given your heritage."

"Given our freedom."

In the past of Utopia, in the Age of Confusion, Mr. Barnstaple
had to remember, everyone had grown up with a crippled or a
thwarted will, hampered by vain restrictions or misled by plausible
delusions. Utopia still bore it in mind that human nature was
fundamentally animal and savage and had to be adapted to social
needs, but Utopia had learnt the better methods of adaptation –
after endless failures of compulsion, cruelty and deception. "On
Earth we tame our animals with hot irons and our fellow men by
violence and fraud," said Mr. Barnstaple, and described the schools
and books, newspapers and public discussions of the early
twentieth-century to his incredulous companions. "You cannot imagine how beaten and fearful even decent people are upon Earth. You
learn of the Age of Confusion in your histories but you do not know

what the realities of a bad mental atmosphere, an atmosphere of feeble laws, hates and superstitions, are. As night goes round the Earth always there are hundreds of thousands of people who should be sleeping, lying awake, fearing a bully, fearing a cruel competition, dreading lest they cannot make good, ill of some illness they cannot comprehend, distressed by some thwarted instinct or some suppressed and perverted desire.". . .

Crystal admitted that it was hard to think now of the Age of Confusion in terms of misery. Much of the everyday misery of Earth was now inconceivable. Very slowly Utopia had evolved its present harmony of law and custom and education. Man was no longer crippled and compelled; it was recognized that he was fundamentally an animal and that his daily life must follow the round of appetites satisfied and instinct released. The daily texture of Utopian life was woven of various and interesting foods and drinks, of free and entertaining exercise and work, of sweet sleep and of the interest and happiness of fearless and spiteless love-making. Inhibition was at a minimum. But where the power of Utopian education began was after the animal had been satisfied and disposed of. The jewel òn the reptile's head that had brought Utopia out of the confusions of human life was curiosity, the play impulse, prolonged and expanded in adult life into an insatiable appetite for knowledge and an habitual creative urgency. All Utopians had become as little children, learners and makers.

It was strange to hear this boy speaking so plainly and clearly of the educational process to which he was being subjected, and particularly to find he could talk so frankly of love.

An earthly bashfulness almost prevented Mr. Barnstaple from asking, "But you –. You do not make Love?"

"I have had curiosities," said the boy, evidently saying what he had been taught to say. "But it is not necessary nor becoming to make love too early in life nor to let desire take hold of one. It weakens youth to become too early possessed by desire – which often will not leave one again. It spoils and cripples the imagination. I want to do good work as my father has done before me."

Mr. Barnstaple glanced at the beautiful young profile at his side and was suddenly troubled by memories of a certain study number four at school, and of some ugly phases of his adolescence, the stuffy, secret room, the hot and ugly fact. He felt a beastlier Earthling than ever. "Heighho!" he sighed. "But this world of yours is as clean as starlight and as sweet as cold water on a dusty day."

"Many people I love," said the boy, "but not with passion. Some day that will come. But one must not be too eager and anxious to meet passionate love or one might make-believe and give or snatch at a sham. . . . There is no hurry. No one will prevent me when my times comes. All good things come to one in this world in their own good time."

But work one does not wait for; one's work, since it concerns one's own self only, one goes to meet. Crystal thought very much about the work he might do. It seemed to Mr. Barnstaple that work, in the sense of uncongenial toil, had almost disappeared from Utopia. Yet all Utopia was working. Everyone was doing work that fitted natural aptitudes and appealed to the imagination of the worker. Everyone worked happily and eagerly — as those people we call geniuses do on our Earth.

. . . .

Crystal was still of an age to be proud of his _savoir faire_. He showed Mr. Barnstaple his books and told him of his tutors and exercises.

Utopia still made use of printed books; books were still the simplest, clearest way of bringing statements before a tranquil mind. Crystal's books were very beautifully bound in flexible leather that his mother had tooled for him very prettily, and they were made of hand-made paper. The lettering was some fluent phonetic script that Mr. Barnstaple could not understand. It reminded him of Arabic; and frequent sketches, outline maps and diagrams were interpolated. Crystal was advised in his holiday reading by a tutor for whom he prepared a sort of exercise report, and he supplemented his reading by visits to museums; but there was no educational museum convenient in the Valley of Peace for Mr. Barnstaple to visit.

Crystal had passed out of the opening stage of education which was carried on, he said, upon large educational estates given up wholly to the lives of children. Education up to eleven or twelve seemed to be much more carefully watched and guarded and taken care of in Utopia than upon earth. Shocks to the imagination, fear and evil suggestions were warded off as carefully as were infection and physical disaster; by eight or nine the foundations of a Utopian character were surely laid, habits of cleanliness, truth, candor and helpfulness, confidence in the world, fearlessness and a sense of belonging to the great purpose of the race.

Only after nine or ten did the child go outside the garden of its early growth and begin to see the ordinary ways of the world. Until that age the care of the children was largely in the hands of nurses *and teachers, but after that time the parents became more of a factor than they had been in a youngster's life. It was always a custom for the parents of a child to be near and to see that child in its nursery days, but just when earthly parents tended to separate from their children as they went away to school or went into business, Utopian parentage grew to be something closer. There was an idea in Utopia that between parent and child there was a necessary temperamental sympathy; children looked forward to the friendship and company of their parents, and parents looked forward to the interest of their children's adolescence, and though a parent had practically no power over a son or daughter, he or she took naturally the position of advocate, adviser and sympathetic friend. The friendship was all the franker and closer because of that lack of power, and all the easier because age for age the Utopians were so much younger and fresher-minded than Earthlings.*

. . . .

Every young Utopian had to learn the Five Principles of Liberty, without which civilization is impossible. The first was the Principle of Privacy. This is that all individual personal facts are private between the citizen and the public organization to which he entrusts them, and can be used only for his convenience and with his sanction. Of course all such facts are available for statistical uses, but not as individual personal facts. And the second principle is the Principle of Free Movement. A Citizen, subject to the due discharge of his public obligations, may go without permission or explanation to any part of the Utopian planet. All the means of transport are freely at his service. Every Utopian may change his surroundings, his climate and his social atmosphere as he will. The third principle is the Principle of Unlimited Knowledge. All that is known in Utopia, except individual personal facts about living people, is on record and as easily available as a perfected series of indices, libraries, museums, and inquiry offices can make it. Whatever the Utopian desires to know he may know with the utmost clearness, exactness and facility so far as his powers of knowing and his industry go. Nothing is kept from him and nothing is misrepresented to him. And that brought Mr. Barnstaple to the fourth Principle of Liberty, which was that Lying is the Blackest Crime.

Crystal's definition of lying was a sweeping one; the inexact statement of facts, even the suppression of a material fact, was lying.

"Where there are lies there cannot be freedom."

Mr. Barnstaple was mightily taken by this idea. It seemed at once quite fresh to him and one that he had always unconsciously entertained. Half the difference between Utopia and our world he asserted lay in this, that our atmosphere was dense and poisonous with lies and shams.

"When one comes to think of it," said Mr. Barnstaple, and began to expatiate to Crystal upon all the falsehoods of human life. The fundamental assumptions of earthly associations were still largely lies, false assumptions of necessary and unavoidable differences in flags and nationality, pretences of function and power in monarchy; impostures of organized learning, religious and moral dogmas and shams. And one must live in it; one is a part of it. You are restrained, taxed, distressed and killed by these insane unrealities. "Lying the Primary Crime! How simple that is! How true and necessary it is! That dogma is the fundamental distinction of the scientific world-state from all preceding states." And going on from that Mr. Barnstaple launched out into a long and loud tirade against the suppression and falsifications of earthly newspapers.

It was a question very near his heart. The London newspapers had ceased to be impartial vehicles of news; they omitted, they mutilated, they misstated. They were no better than propaganda rags. Rags! <u>Nature</u>, within its field, was shiningly accurate and full, but that was a purely scientific paper; it did not touch the everyday news. The Press, he held, was the only possible salt of contemporary life, and if the salt had lost its savor — !

The poor man found himself orating as though he was back at his Sydenham breakfast-table after a bad morning's paper.

"Once upon a time Utopia was in just such a tangle," said Crystal consolingly. "But there is a proverb, 'Truth comes back where once she has visited.' You need not trouble so much as you do. Someday even your press may grow clear."

"How do <u>you</u> manage about newspapers and criticism?" said Mr. Barnstaple.

Crystal explained that there was a complete distinction between news and discussion in Utopia. There were houses — one was in sight — which were used as reading-rooms. One went to these places to learn the news. Thither went the reports of all the things that were happening on the planet, things found, things discovered, things done. The reports were made as they were needed; there were no advertisement contracts to demand the same bulk of news every day. For some time Crystal said the reports had been very full and amusing about the Earthlings, but he had not been reading the paper *for many days because of the interest in history the Earthling affair had aroused in him. There was always news of fresh scientific discoveries that stirred the imagination. One frequent item of public interest and excitement was the laying out of some wide scheme of research. The new spatial work that Arden and Greenlake had died for was producing much news. And when people died in Utopia it was the custom to tell the story of their lives. Crystal promised to take Mr. Barnstaple to a news place and entertain him by reading him some of the Utopian descriptions of earthly life which had been derived from the Earthlings, and Mr. Barnstaple asked that when this was done he might also hear about Arden and Greenlake, who had been not only great discoverers, but great lovers, and of Serpentine and Cedar, for whom he had conceived an intense admiration. Utopian news lacked of course the high spice of an earthly newspaper; the intriguing murders and amusing behaviors, the entertaining and exciting consequences of sexual ignorance and sexual blunderings, the libel cases and detected swindles, the great processional movements of Royalty across the general traffic, and the romantic fluctuations of the stock exchange and sport. But where the news of Utopia lacked liveliness, the liveliness of discussion made up for it. For the Fifth Principle of Liberty in Utopia was Free Discussion and Criticism.*

Any Utopian was free to criticize and discuss anything in the whole universe provided he told no lies about it directly or indirectly; he could propose anything however subversive. He could break into poetry or fiction as he chose. He could express himself in any literary form he liked or by sketch or caricature as the mood took him. Only he must refrain from lying; that was the one rigid rule of controversy. He could get what he had to say printed and distributed to the news rooms. There it was read or neglected as the visitors chanced to approve of it or not. Often if they liked what they read they would carry off a copy with them. Crystal had some new fantastic fiction about the exploration of space among his books; imaginative stories that boys were reading very eagerly; they were pamphlets of thirty or forty pages printed on a beautiful paper that he said was made directly from flax and certain reeds. The librarians noted what books and papers were read and taken away, and these they replaced with fresh copies. The piles that went unread were presently reduced to one or two copies and the rest went back to the pulping mills. But many of the poets and philosophers and story-tellers whose imaginations found no wide popularity were nevertheless treasured and their memories kept alive by a few devoted admirers.

Chapter Twelve

ALDOUS HUXLEY AND *BRAVE NEW WORLD*

Like Butler's *Erewhon*, Aldous Huxley's *Brave New World* is a satiric utopian work. Unlike *Erewhon*, however, Huxley propounds an extremely negative kind of society. The Erewhonians were backward and boring, but likeable. In *Brave New World* we find a highly intellectualized and progressive kind of society that is often cruel and heartless. It is the kind of world that devotees of the cinema would understand as a world developed and controlled by "mad" scientists.

Huxley's writings reveal the accumulation of vast stores of information which he can express to the reader in a very palpable form, through fiction as well as nonfiction. In his lifetime, he sought constantly to sift through the bulk of human knowledge in order to present a synthesization of it. Sometimes this synthesization revealed itself in the form of an attack on the church, or democratic society, or other institutionalized forms of life. Huxley refused to accept secondhand philosophy, government, or religion. He was a skeptic who challenged the knowledge and beliefs and social myths which so many of us live by. As Syndey Thompson put it:

> *To be a Huxley is to be a revolutionary. For a century the name of Huxley has been associated with revolt: revolt against assumed authority, against orthodox religion and against the accepted conventions of the day. Aldous has not escaped the family tendency. A true satirist, he is at bottom less interested in lampooning someone or something for the mere sake of it than he is in expressing something lying deep in his nature.*[1]

Like his famous grandfather, Thomas Henry Huxley, and his brother Julian, Aldous is very much interested in science. He is also capable of handling and developing scientific studies in a very adroit and original manner. *Brave New World,* with its Hatcheries and Conditioning Center, as well as its Electro-magnetic Golf, show this ability at its best.

[1]Sydney Thompson, "Aldous Huxley," *Humberside,* 3:247-259, October, 1930.

As a writer, Huxley is bound neither by taboos nor by superficial enchantments. He does not see science as a sacred cow, any more than he does religion or government. If anything, he presents the picture of an author who is continually searching for the truth, and all knowledge becomes grist for the mill. He once wrote a book whose title sums up the theme of this sketch, a book called *Jesting Pilate.* Just as Pilate asked, in jest, "What is Truth?" so too, Huxley continues to ask this same question and seems to reply at times that perhaps there is no truth.

Huxley makes the point in *Ends and Means* that man is not only affected by his past (the Freudian approach) but also by what he sees in the future. He believed that we are living in parlous times, and that the type of future which we envision has a great deal to do with the type of future which we probably will have. The difficulty which most men have in seeing a future in which love, truth, and justice prevail has a great deal to do with the reason why men are so fearful and anxious about coming events, according to Huxley. Thus, in *Brave New World,* he is speaking for every man. He presents a threatening, but a not impossible world to come. Indeed, many would contend that this is probably what the world of the future will be, judging by our present direction.

Many of Huxley's followers have taken *Brave New World,* with all of its mechanized tortures, to be a refutation of the world of the machine, and a vindication of the doctrines of Rousseau, as well as those of Morris and Butler. It is not true, however, that Huxley was against technology *per se.* If there was anyone who was anxious to promote advancements in technology and science, it was Aldous Huxley. What he did object to, however, was the overdependence of men on machines. He felt that the machines could destroy basic creative human impulses unless a balance was found between what the machine could do best and what man could do best.

The growing problem for Huxley, which is even more acute today, is how man shall spend his leisure time. Man's leisure, Huxley believed, was becoming just as mechanized as his work life. In *Do What You Will,* he has a great deal to say about that large body of people who no longer amuse themselves creatively, but sit around and are passively amused by mechanical devices. He was speaking then about motion pictures. How much greater would his concern be now, since the development and proliferation of TV.

Seventeen years after the publication of *Brave New World* George Orwell wrote another satirical and negative utopian work, a dysutopia entitled *1984.* In *1984,* like *Brave New World,* we are shown a world in which machines are men's enemies, rather than their friends. There are telescreens which are used by the Thought Police to view individuals during their entire waking life, as well as processes for vaporizing people whom the government (Big Brother) considers undesirable. In both of these works, *Brave New World* and *1984,* we are presented with terrifying worlds that men have either desired or let happen to them. The most terrifying thing of all, perhaps, is that these worlds are now within the range of possibility. We got a taste of it during the reign of Adolph Hitler, and there are still places in the world today where mechanized contrivances, as well as science, have conspired to prevent man's achieving freedom, and have also succeeded in thwarting any feelings of brotherhood he might have.

In *1984,* education is controlled by the Ministry of Truth. It is here that history is rewritten in a day-to-day falsification of the past in order to show that the events of history have always supported the party in power. It is in the Ministry of Truth, also, where student textbooks are carefully doctored, and where the English language is constantly being revised and shortened to create a language known as *Newspeak.*

One of the most important of all the developments in *1984* is known as doublethink (the power of holding two contradictory beliefs in one's mind simultaneously, and accepting both of them. It is through doublethink that all knowledge can be neutralized. A party intellectual can know that he is playing tricks with reality, and yet not really believe that he is. This mental cheating allows one to accept and, at the same time, reject every kind of social and scientific principle. The party might say, for example, "that ice is heavier than water," or "that two and two make five." The ability to double-think, as well as to exercise crimestop (the development of a blind spot in the mind whenever a dangerous idea presents itself) are necessary requirements in order to survive in this new world. Those who are not able to develop these abilities, due either to bad training or poor conditioning, leave themselves open to commiting the worst of all evils in 1984 — thoughtcrime.

Nor is education neglected in the *Brave New World* that Huxley creates. It is one of the most central of concepts, and for that very reason is directly under the control of science. No longer do students have to worry about the arduous task of learning, as in *1984.* Now, learning is "built in" from birth, and the student knows what he is supposed to know, *i.e.,* what is befitting to his ordained station in life. Like *1984,* this too, is a highly controlled society, and science has perhaps become even more frightening in this work. Children are factory-made on an assembly line of test tubes and incubators.

Through the use of genetically conditioned sperm and ova, as well as through the use of chemicals for a dulling effect, the mentality of an individual can be prepared to order.

In *1984,* a few individuals found it possible to escape the indoctrination process which warped men's minds, but in *Brave New World* only those outside the range of civilized society, the primitives, are allowed to escape. It is scientific breeding (Bokanovsky's Process) which can now create uniform batches of Alphas, Betas, Gammas, Deltas, and Epsilons, with a scale of descending intelligence in that order. For the first time, according to the leaders of *Brave New World,* man has achieved absolute social stability. Now, men can not only be made for the jobs which the state desires them to have, but they can also be conditioned to enjoy only that kind of work.

In writing satirical works, one only satirizes what is important to him. It may not be a pleasant subject, but at least it is one which to the author deserves great concern. This is exemplified in Huxley's treatment of education. He satirizes education because it is an important aspect of life to him. This importance is further shown by the attention which he gives to twentieth-century education in some of his other writings. In an essay entitled "The Education of an Amphibian," he tells what he thinks about the present state of organized education.

> *Whether we like it or not, we are amphibians, living simultaneously in the world of experience and the world of notions, in the world of direct apprehension of Nature, God and ourselves, and the world of abstract, verbalized knowledge about these primary facts. Our business as human beings is to make the best of both these worlds.*

> *Unfortunately, organized education has done very little, hitherto, to help us in this task. For organized education is predominantly verbal education. . . . Exponents of Progressive Education probably think they are already doing everything that can be done. Under the influence of John Dewey, they have stressed the importance of nonverbal activity as a means of learning. History, for example, is now often taught in a series of "projects." Stonehenge is reconstructed with brickbats in the back yard. Life in the Middle Ages is dramatically reproduced — minus, of course, the dirt, the violence and the theology, which were the essence of that life. Whether children learn more through these mud-pie techniques of education than they would learn by being shown pictures and reading an intelligent book, I do not profess to know. The important point, in our present context, is that the "doing," through which the children are supposed to learn, is left unanalyzed by the Progressive Edu-*

cators who advocate it. So far as they are concerned, doing is doing; there is nothing to choose between one kind of doing and another. John Dewey himself knew better; but his followers have chosen to ignore his qualifications of the learning-by-doing doctrine and to plunge headlong and with unquestioning enthusiasm into their mud pies.[2]

In this same essay, Huxley goes on to point out that "learning-by-doing" is a sound principle only when the doing is good doing. Most of the time, he thinks, the learning is bad doing. In another essay, entitled "Knowledge and Understanding," he continues his attack on what he considers the misuse of Dewey's principles.

Professional educationists have taken John Dewey's theories of "learning through doing" and of "education as life-adjustment," and have applied them in such a way that, in many American schools, there is now doing without learning, along with courses in adjustment to everything except the basic twentieth-century fact that we live in a world where ignorance of science and its methods is the surest, shortest road to national disaster.[3]

In the following selections from *Brave New World*, there is no further talk about professional educationists, nor about the need for values in human life (a subject of great concern to Huxley). Instead, we are shown, after all our frustrations about education, government, religion, *etc.*, what is *fait accompli*. We are shown what happens to a human society that promotes false values, which ultimately, causes people to accept or create conditions which result in a curtailment of basic human freedoms.

BRAVE NEW WORLD - Aldous Huxley*

In the following selections, the author describes the educational processes in a rather frightening Utopia, projected six hundred and thirty-two years into the future. A.F. 632 (six hundred and thirty-two years after Ford) to be exact. In this monstrous caricature of the future world, even science is subjected to the intellectual cynicism of a writer who forsees education in the new world conducted along lines of Ford-plant efficiency.

[2]Aldous Huxley, *Tomorrow and Tomorrow and Tomorrow (and Other Essays)*, (New York: Harper and Brothers, 1952), pp. 7-9.
[3]*Ibid.*, p. 40.
*Aldous Huxley, *Brave New World* (New York: Bantam Books, 1932), pp. 2-4, 12-15, 17-19.

"I shall begin at the beginning," said the D. H. C. *[Director of Hatcheries and Conditioning]* and the more zealous students recorded his intention in their notebooks: *Begin at the beginning.* *"These,"* he waved his hand, *"are the incubators."* And opening an insulated door he showed them racks upon racks of numbered test-tubes. *"The week's supply of ova. Kept,"* he explained, *"at blood heat; whereas the male gametes,"* and here he opened another door, *"they have to be kept at thirty-five instead of thirty-seven. Full blood heat sterilizes."* Rams wrapped in thermogene beget no lambs.

Still leaning against the incubators he gave them, while the pencils scurried illegibly across the pages, a brief description of the modern fertilizing process; spoke first, of course, of its surgical introduction — *"the operation undergone voluntarily for the good of Society, not to mention the fact that it carries a bonus amounting to six months' salary"*; continued with some account of the technique for preserving the excised ovary alive and actively developing; passed on to a consideration of optimum temperature, salinity, viscoscity; referred to the liquor in which the detached and ripened eggs were kept; and, leading his charges to the work tables, actually showed them how this liquor was drawn off from the test-tubes; how it was let out drop by drop onto the specially warmed slides of the microscopes; how the eggs which it contained were inspected for abnormalities, counted and transferred to a porous receptacle; how (and he now took them to watch the operation) this receptacle was immersed in a warm bouillon containing free-swimming spermatozoa — at a minimum concentration of one hundred thousand per cubic centimeter, he insisted; and how, after ten minutes, the container was lifted out of the liquor, and its contents reexamined; how, if any of the eggs remained unfertilized, it was again immersed, and, if necessary, yet again; how the fertilized ova went back to the incubators; where the Alphas and Betas remained until definitely bottled; while the Gammas, Deltas and Epsilons were brought out again, after only thirty-six hours, to undergo Bokanovsky's Process.

"Bokanovsky's Process," repeated the Director, and the students underlined the words in their little notebooks.

One egg, one embryo, one adult — normality. But a bokanovskified egg will bud, will proliferate, will divide. From eight to ninety-six buds, and every bud will grow into a perfectly formed embryo, and every embryo into a full-sized adult. Making ninety-six human beings grow where only one grew before. Progress.

"Essentially," the D.H.C. concluded, *"bokanovskification consists of a series of arrests of development. We check the normal growth and, paradoxically enough, the egg responds by budding."*

Responds by budding. The pencils were busy.

He pointed. On a very slowly moving band a rack-full of test-tubes was entering a large metal box, another rack-full was emerging. Machinery faintly purred. It took eight minutes for the tubes to go through, he told them. Eight minutes of hard X-rays being about as much as an egg can stand. A few died; of the rest, the least susceptible divided into two; most put out four buds; some eight; all were returned to the incubators, where the buds began to develop; then, after two days, were suddenly chilled, chilled and checked. Two, four, eight, the buds in their turn budded; and having budded were dosed almost to death with alcohol; consequently burgeoned again and having budded — bud out of bud out of bud — were thereafter — further arrest being generally fatal — left to develop in peace. By which time the original egg was in a fair way to becoming anything from eight to ninety-six embryos — a prodigious improvement, you will agree, on nature. Identical twins — but not in piddling twos or threes as in the old viviparous days, when an egg would sometimes accidently divide; actually by dozens, by scores at a time.

"Scores," the Director repeated and flung out his arms as though he were distributing largesse. "Scores."

But one of the students was fool enough to ask where the advantage lay.

"My good boy!" The Director wheeled sharply round on him. "Can't you see? Can't you see?" He raised a hand; his expression was solemn. "Bokanovsky's Process is one of the major instruments of social stability!"

Major instruments of social stability.

Standard men and women; in uniform batches. The whole of a small factory staffed with the products of a single bokanovskified egg.

"Ninety-six identical twins working ninety-six identical machines!" The voice was almost tremulous with enthusiasm. "You really know where you are. For the first time in history." He quoted the planetary motto. "Community, Identity, Stability." Grand words. "If we could bokanovskify indefinitely the whole problem would be solved."

Solved by standard Gammas, unvarying Deltas, uniform Epsilons. Millions of identical twins. The principle of mass production at last applied to biology.

The D.H.C. and his students stepped into the nearest lift and were carried up to the fifth floor.

INFANT NURSERIES. NEO-PAVLOVIAN CONDITIONING ROOMS, announced the notice board.

The Director opened a door. They were in a large bare room, very bright and sunny; for the whole of the southern wall was a single window. Half a dozen nurses, trousered and jacketed in the regulation white viscose-linen uniform, their hair aseptically hidden under white caps, were engaged in setting out bowls of roses in a long row across the floor. Big bowls, packed tight with blossom. Thousands of petals, ripe-blown and silkily smooth, like the cheeks of innumerable little cherubs, but of cherubs, in that bright light, not exclusively pink and Aryan, but also luminously Chinese, also Mexican, also apoplectic with too much blowing of celestial trumpets, also pale as death, pale with the posthumous whiteness of marble.

The nurses stiffened to attention as the D.H.C. came in.

"Set out the books," he said curtly.

In silence the nurses obeyed his command. Between the rose bowls the books were duly set out — a row of nursery quartos opened invitingly each at some gaily colored image of beast or fish or bird.

"Now bring in the children."

They hurried out of the room and returned in a minute or two, each pushing a kind of tall dumb-waiter laden, on all its four wire-netted shelves, with eight-month-old babies, all exactly alike (a Bokanovsky Group, it was evident) and all (since their caste was Delta) dressed in khaki.

"Put them down on the floor."

The infants were unloaded.

"Now turn them so that they can see the flowers and books."

Turned, the babies at once fell silent, then began to crawl towards those clusters of sleek colors, those shapes so gay and brilliant on the white pages. As they approached, the sun came out of a momentary eclipse behind a cloud. The roses flamed up as though with a sudden passion from within; a new and profound significance seemed to suffuse the shining pages of the books. From the ranks of the crawling babies came little squeals of excitement, gurgles and twitterings of pleasure.

The Director rubbed his hands. "Excellent!" he said. "It might almost have been done on purpose."

The swiftest crawlers were already at their goal. Small hands reached out uncertainly, touched, grasped, unpetaling the trans-

figured roses, crumpling the illuminated pages of the books. The Director waited until all were happily busy. Then, "Watch carefully," he said. And, lifting his hand, he gave the signal.

The Head Nurse, who was standing by a switchboard at the other end of the room, pressed down a little lever.

There was a violent explosion. Shriller and ever shriller, a siren shrieked. Alarm bells maddeningly sounded.

The children started, screamed; their faces were distorted with terror.

"And now," the Director shouted (for the noise was deafening), "now we proceed to rub in the lesson with a mild electric shock."

He waved his hand again, and the Head Nurse pressed a second lever. The screaming of the babies suddenly changed its tone. There was something desperate, almost insane, about the sharp spasmodic yelps to which they now gave utterance. Their little bodies twitched and stiffened; their limbs moved jerkily as if to the tug of unseen wires.

"We can electrify that whole strip of floor," bawled the Director in explanation. "But that's enough," he signalled to the nurse.

The explosions ceased, the bells stopped ringing, the shriek of the siren died down from tone to tone into silence. The stiffly twitching bodies relaxed, and what had become the sob and yelp of infant maniacs broadened out once more into a normal howl of ordinary terror.

"Offer them the flowers and the books again."

The nurses obeyed; but at the approach of the roses, at the mere sight of those gaily-colored images of pussy and cock-a-doodle-doo and baa-baa black sheep, the infants shrank away in horror; the volume of the howling suddenly increased.

Books and loud noises, flowers and electric shocks — already in the infant mind these couples were compromisingly linked; and after two hundred repetitions of the same or a similar lesson would be wedded indissolubly. What man has joined, nature is powerless to put asunder.

"They'll grow up with what the psychologists used to call an 'instinctive' hatred of books and flowers. Reflexes unalterably conditioned. They'll be safe from books and botany all their lives." The Director turned to his nurses. "Take them away again."

Still yelling, the khaki babies were loaded on to their dumb-waiters and wheeled out, leaving behind them the smell of sour milk and a most welcome silence.

One of the students held up his hand; and though he could see quite well why you couldn't have lower-caste people wasting the Community's time over books, and that there was always the risk of their reading something which might undersirably decondition one of their reflexes, yet. . .well, he couldn't understand about the flowers. Why go to the trouble of making it psychologically impossible for Deltas to like flowers?

Patiently the D.H.C. explained. If the children were made to scream at the sight of a rose, that was on grounds of high economic policy. Not so very long ago (a century or thereabouts), Gammas, Deltas, even Epsilons, had been conditioned to like flowers — flowers in particular and wild nature in general. The idea was to make them want to be going out into the country at every available opportunity, and so compel them to consume transport.

"And didn't they consume transport?" asked the student.

"Quite a lot," the D.H.C. replied. "But nothing else."

Primroses and landscapes, he pointed out, have one grave defect: they are gratuitous. A love of nature keeps no factories busy. It was decided to abolish the love of nature, at any rate among the lower classes; to abolish the love of nature, but not the tendency to consume transport. For of course it was essential that they should keep on going to the country, even though they hated it. The problem was to find an economically sounder reason for consuming transport than a mere affection for primroses and landscapes. It was duly found.

"We condition the masses to hate the country," concluded the Director. "But simultaneously we condition them to love all country sports. At the same time, we see to it that all country sports shall entail the use of elaborate apparatus. So that they consume manufactured articles as well as transport. Hence those electric shocks."

"I see," said the student, and was silent, lost in admiration.

. . . .

Fifty yards of tiptoeing brought them to a door which the Director cautiously opened. They stepped over the threshold into the twilight of a shuttered dormitory. Eighty cots stood in a row against the wall. There was a sound of light regular breathing and a continuous murmur, as of very faint voices remotely whispering.

A nurse rose as they entered and came to attention before the Director.

"What's the lesson this afternoon?" he asked.

"We had Elementary Sex for the first forty minutes," she answered. "But now it's switched over to Elementary Class Consciousness."

The Director walked slowly down the long line of cots. Rosy and relaxed with sleep, eighty little boys and girls lay softly breathing. There was a whisper under every pillow. The D.H.C. halted and, bending over one of the little beds, listened attentively.

"Elementary Class Consciousness, did you say? Let's have it repeated a little louder by the trumpet."

At the end of the room a loud speaker projected from the wall. The Director walked up to it and pressed a switch.

" . .all wear green," said a soft but very distinct voice, beginning in the middle of a sentence, "and Delta children wear khaki. Oh no, I don't want to play with Delta children. And Epsilons are still worse. They're too stupid to be able to read or write. Besides they wear black, which is such a beastly color. I'm so glad I'm a Beta."

There was a pause; then the voice began again.

"Alpha children wear grey. They work much harder than we do, because they're so frightfully clever. I'm really awfully glad I'm a Beta, because I don't work so hard. And then we are much better than the Gammas and Deltas. Gammas are stupid. They all wear green, and Delta children wear khaki. Oh no, I don't want to play with Delta children. And Epsilons are still worse. They're too stupid to be able. . . . "

The Director pushed back the switch. The voice was silent. Only its thin ghost continued to mutter from beneath the eighty pillows.

"They'll have that repeated forty or fifty times more before they wake; then again on Thursday, and again on Saturday. A hundred and twenty times three times a week for thirty months. After which they go on to a more advanced lesson."

Roses and electric shocks, the khaki of Deltas and a whiff of asafoetida — wedded indissolubly before the child can speak. But wordless conditioning is crude and wholesale; cannot bring home the finer distinctions, cannot inculcate the more complex courses of behavior. For that there must be words, but words without reason. In brief, hynopaedia.

"The greatest moralizing and socializing force of all time."

The students took it down in their little books. Straight from the Horse's mouth.

Once more the Director touched the switch.

". . .so frightfully clever," the soft, insinuating, indefatigable voice was saying, "I'm really awfully glad I'm a Beta, because. . . "

Not so much like drops of water, though water, it is true, can wear holes in the hardest granite; rather, drops of liquid sealing-wax, drops that adhere, incrust, incorporate themselves with what they fall on, till finally the rock is all one scarlet blob.

"Till at last the child's mind is these suggestions, and the sum of the suggestions is the child's mind. And not the child's mind only. The adult's mind — all his life long. The mind that judges and desires and decides — made up of these suggestions. But all these suggestions are our suggestions!" The Director almost shouted in his triumph. "Suggestions from the State." He banged the nearest table. "It therefore follows. . . ."

A noise made him turn around.

"Oh, Ford!" he said in another tone. "I've gone and woken the children."

Chapter Thirteen

B. F. SKINNER AND
WALDEN TWO

Walden Two is an engrossing novel in many ways. To begin with, it is unusual in that it is a book of fiction done by an eminent psychologist. Only a few academicians have shown themselves capable of writing well in both fiction and nonfiction. Skinner is an exception to this rule.

It is quite significant that Skinner calls this book *Walden Two,* patterning its title after Thoreau's *Walden,* even though there are many significant differences between the two. *Walden* is the nonfictional account of a man living a solitary existence in and among nature. In *Walden Two* we have a large group of men and women, living harmoniously, to be sure, but within a highly complex and mechanized society. The kind of life that persons such as Thoreau and Rosseau recognized as corrupting to man's soul has reached its peak in *Walden Two.* Instead of corrupting man, however, economic and political security, as well as brotherhood, go hand in hand in the world which Skinner describes.

Skinner believes that the planned existence which people have in *Walden Two* is really conducive to their best interests. This is not only the kind of life which is most natural and beneficial to man, but also the kind which will make him the happiest. Skinner pictures man enjoying this scientific culture as much as did Thoreau his small tract of woods.

Skinner's proposals for leading the "good" life seem to be more realistic than those of Thoreau, for we cannot possibly return to the life of simplicity and natural living which he enjoyed in the middle-nineteenth century. It is necessary today that man learn how to live with his machines, and Skinner does offer one solution as to how this might be done.

Skinner has consciously written down to his readers in this book, which was designed for a wider audience than his technical writings; and thus one finds a great disparity between the language, of say, *Science and Human Behavior,* and *Walden Two,* even when they are both discussing the same thing, such as reinforcement theory. In *Walden Two,* Skinner speaks of reinforcement as a method whereby certain goals are obtained without compulsion or distaste. He does not elaborate on either the meaning or the development of these theories toward which he personally contributed a significant amount of research. He speaks about them as *faits accomplis* in *Walden Two,* and as an accepted feature of man's social development.

Anyone not familiar with Professor Skinner's past achievements, especially his work on pigeons and with teaching machines in the development of reinforcement theory, would probably not recognize this book as one done by a psychologist. No effort is made to include psychological jargon, nor to talk of psychology as a special field of inquiry to the exclusion of other fields of study. The emphasis in this work is on the socio-political life of man, and psychology and reinforcement theories are only important in so far as they promote this kind of development. This is, I feel, an important point to stress, *i.e.,* that the author has a definite opinion at all times of what man should do, and where he should go. We hear, for example, so often from people in the sciences, especially, that they are not concerned with the uses or ends of their scientific achievements — that they are only interested in science. The atomic bomb is a sad commentary upon where this type of thinking leads us. Skinner is concerned that psychology be developed not as an abstract discipline but as an aid to man in his search for development and, most of all, in his search for happiness. Throughout *Walden Two* the emphasis is on happiness; and conditioning, learning, and other features are considered useful only when they lead toward this pursuit of happiness. As regards learning, one is reminded here of Morris' *News from Nowhere,* where learning the traditional subject-matter taught in the schools is not valued highly because it does not lead to happiness. Skinner speaks, for example, of history in this fashion, pointing out that history is read in Walden Two, but is not studied.

Skinner makes an important distinction between what he calls "cultural engineering" and what one might call "noncultural engineering." In the former, mechanical improvements are developed for the specific purpose of raising the cultural standards of the community. There are no gadgets in *Walden Two,* even though one might be inclined to rate his method of engineered tea service as such. Yet, this is considered only as an efficient way of arranging tea so that time may be saved and conditions made satisfactory for the more important things, such as the conversation and the planning which goes on at such sessions. Skinner objects strongly to the misuse of technological skill in our culture in order to create an abundancy of such mechanical devices as automatic back-scratchers and stereophonic rock 'n' roll, which do nothing to raise the cultural standards of the community and may, indeed, lower them. One technique which Skinner points to as an example of cultural engineering is the creation of air-conditioned cubicles in which newborn babies are kept, receiving moist air at a temperature between 88 and 90 degrees. In *Cumulative Record,* Skinner tells how he has adopted this technique, which he now calls an Air Crib, for the rearing of his own child.[1]

There is no money in Walden Two. All goods and services are free and may be purchased with labor credits. Each person is required to work four hours every day and for this amount of work receives four labor credits. It is on this basis that goods and services are distributed. If a particular job is such an unpleasant one that there are not many who wish to do it, then for such jobs one and a half credits are given for each hour, instead of the usual one credit; whereas excessively pleasant jobs, such as working in flower gardens, are given less than the average number of credits.

The dialectic, which consists largely of a series of discussions between Frazier, the creator of Walden Two, and Professor Burris (Skinner's first name is Burrhus) who goes to visit him, is used interestingly throughout the book. Take, for example, the time when Professor Burris begins to argue that the children of Walden Two, when exposed to the outside world, the night clubs, fancy restaurants, or homes of the rich, will feel a twinge of envy, and then perhaps doubt whether Walden Two is the best kind of society after all. Frazier replies that the only way to protect them from this feeling is to tell them not partial truths about this outside world, but the whole truth – to show them not only the fine residences and museums but also the saloons, the jails, and the City Hospitals.

> *Once in a while we give a group of children a sort of detective assignment. The game is to establish a connection in the shortest possible time between any given bit of luxury and some piece of depravity. The children may start with a fine residence, for example. By going in the service drive they may be able to speak to a colored laundress hanging out clothes. They induce her to let them drive her home. That's enough. Or they pick out some shabby figure leaving a cathedral and follow him to the less exalted surroundings in which he spends most of his day.*[2]

[1] B. F. Skinner, *Cumulative Record* (New York: Appleton-Century-Crofts, Inc., 1959), p. 419ff.

[2] B. F. Skinner, *Walden Two* (New York: The Macmillan Company, 1948), p. 172.

Indoctrination, therefore, according to Frazier, is not as safe an instrument as the truth. However, there is such a thing as controlling behavior, which is practiced in Walden Two. When Professor Burris questions this on the basis of freedom, Frazier replies that we can not only control behavior, but that we must. Frazier explains that in the past, man's behavior was largely controlled by punishment or fear, but that this has never proven very satisfactory. The modern method, he explains, is to use reinforcement. Thus, when a person behaves as we wish him to, we create a situation he likes, or remove one he doesn't like, and thus he consequently tends to behave that way again, resulting in what is called, "positive reinforcement." Frazier points out his belief that this does not limit individual freedom, since people feel that they are doing what they want to do, and not what they are forced to do.

Skinner places education under very sharp focus in many instances. In Chapter Twenty-five, for example, Professor Burris is talking to two ladies who ask him "embarrassing" questions about his work as a college professor. They ask such questions as, Why do colleges make their students take examinations, and why do they give grades? What does a grade really mean? When a student studies, does he do anything more than read and think — or is there something special which no one at Walden Two could know about? Why do the professors lecture to the students? Were the students never expected to do anything except answer questions? Was it true that students are made to read books they are not interested in?

At another place, Professor Burris (expressing what is believed to be Skinner's viewpoint) speaks of the importance of a philosophy of education and of the need for new values, as well as a new conception of man and his place in the scheme of things.

As a teacher I had given little thought to the "philosophy of education." Teaching was a job to be done without benefit of perspective or program. I knew, as all teachers know, that education was inadequately supported. That was perhaps not its own fault, but its outmoded techniques certainly were. Furthermore, education was completely bewildered as to its place in the world of the future. It could inspire no sense of belonging to a movement, no esprit de corps. I could get no satisfaction from atavistic or nostalgic attempts to reconstruct a happier era, and so I contented myself with doing the day's work.

Now, fresh from my experience at Walden Two, I saw that this could not go on. But I also saw that educators themselves could not save the situation. The causes were too deep, too remote. They involved the whole structure of society. What was needed was a new conception of man, compatible with our scientific knowledge, which would lead to a philosophy of education bearing some relation to educational practices. But to achieve this, education would have to abandon the technical limitations which it had imposed upon itself and step forth into a broader sphere of human engineering. Nothing short of the complete revision of a culture would suffice.[3]

Walden Two is an expression of this belief on the part of Skinner that man needs to, and can, step forward into "a broader sphere of human engineering." Skinner rightfully objected to those critics of his book who called it an "ignoble Utopia" or equated it with George Orwell's dire prophecy of *1984*. *Walden Two* is actually the alternative to *1984*, for man does have it within his power today to control behavior, to condition the masses, or to create gigantic feats of engineering skill, which even at times baffle the inventor. The question is, shall these things be used for the purpose of creating a world like *1984* or a world like *Walden Two*. The only thing which can help us from having *1984*, Skinner believes, is to develop within ourselves a continual questioning attitude which asks, "Where are we going? And Why?"

WALDEN TWO – B. F. Skinner*

Professor Burris, Professor Castle, two ex-GI's and their fiancées go to visit an experimental utopian community run by a former fellow graduate student of Professor Burris, named T. E. Frazier. In the following selection, Frazier is explaining the type of education practiced in Walden Two.

The living quarters and daily schedules of the older children furnished a particularly good example of behavioral engineering. At first sight they seemed wholly casual, almost haphazard, but as Frazier pointed out their significant features and the consequences of each, I began to make out a comprehensive, almost Machiavellian design.

The children passed smoothly from one age group to another, following a natural process of growth and avoiding the abrupt changes of the home-and-school system. The arrangements were such that each child emulated children slightly older than himself

[3]B. F. Skinner, *Walden Two* (New York: The Macmillan Company, 1948), pp. 259-260.
    *B. F. Skinner, *Walden Two* (New York: The Macmillan Company, 1948), Chapter 15, pp. 95-104.

and hence derived motives and patterns for much of his early education without adult aid.

The control of the physical and social environment, of which Frazier had made so much, was progressively relaxed – or, to be more exact, the control was transferred from the authorities to the child himself and to the other members of his group. After spending most of the first year in an air-conditioned cubicle, and the second and third mainly in an air-conditioned room with a minimum of clothing and bedding, the three or four-year-old was introduced to regular clothes and given the care of a small standard cot in a dormitory. The beds of the five- and six-year-olds were grouped by threes and fours in a series of alcoves furnished like rooms and treated as such by the children. Groups of three or four seven-year-olds occupied small rooms together, and this practice was continued, with frequent change of roommates, until the children were about thirteen, at which time they took temporary rooms in the adult building, usually in pairs. At marriage, or whenever the individual chose, he could participate in building a larger room for himself or refurnishing an old room which might be available.

A similar withdrawal of supervision, proceeding as rapidly as the child acquired control of himself, could be seen in the dining arrangements. From three through six, the children ate in a small dining room of their own. The older children, as we had observed on our first day at Walden Two, took their meals at specified times in the adult quarters. At thirteen all supervision was abandoned, and the young member was free to eat when and where he pleased.

We visited some of the workshops, laboratories, studies, and reading rooms used in lieu of classrooms. They were occupied, but it was not entirely clear that the children were actually in school. I supposed that the few adults to be seen about the building were teachers, but many of them were men, contrary to my conception of schoolteachers at that age level, and more often than not they were busy with some private business. Since Frazier had requested that we avoid questions or discussions in the presence of the children, we proceeded from one room to another in growing puzzlement. I had to admit that an enormous amount of learning was probably going on, but I had never seen a school like it before.

We inspected a well-equipped gymnasium, a small assembly room, and other facilities. The building was made of rammed earth and very simply decorated, but there was a pleasant "non-institutional" character about it. The doors and many of the windows stood open, and a fair share of the schoolwork, or whatever it was, took place outside. Children were constantly passing in and *out. Although there was an obvious excitement about the place, there was little of the boisterous confusion which develops in the ordinary school when discipline is momentarily relaxed. Everyone seemed to be enjoying extraordinary freedom, but the efficiency and comfort of the whole group were preserved.*

I was reminded of children on good behavior and was on the point of asking how often the pressure reached the bursting point. But there was a difference, too, and my question slowly evaporated. I could only conclude that this happy and productive atmosphere was probably the usual thing. Here again, so far as I could see, Frazier — or someone — had got things under control.

When we returned to our shade tree, I was primed with questions, and so, I am sure, was Castle. But Frazier had other plans. He had either forgotten how remarkable was the spectacle we had just witnessed, or he was intentionally allowing our wonderment and curiosity to ferment. He began from a very different point of view.

"When we discussed the economics of community life," he said, "I should have mentioned education. Teachers are, of course, workers, and I'm willing to defend all that I said about our economic advantage as specifically applied to education. God knows, the outside world is not exactly profligate in the education of its children. It doesn't spend much on equipment or teachers. Yet in spite of this pennywise policy, there's still enormous waste. A much better education would cost less if society were better organized.

"We can arrange things more expeditiously here because we don't need to be constantly re-educating. The ordinary teacher spends a good share of her time changing the cultural and intellectual habits which the child acquires from its family and surrounding culture. Or else the teacher duplicates home training, in a complete waste of time. Here we can almost say that the school is the family, and vice versa.

"We can adopt the best educational methods and still avoid the administrative machinery which schools need in order to adjust to an unfavorable social structure. We don't have to worry about standardization in order to permit pupils to transfer from one school to another, or to appraise or control the work of particular schools. We don't need 'grades.' Everyone knows that talents and abilities don't develop at the same rate in different children. A fourth-grade reader may be a sixth-grade mathematician. The grade is an administrative device which does violence to the nature of the developmental process. Here the child advances as rapidly as he likes in any field. No

time is wasted in forcing him to participate in, or be bored by, activities he has outgrown. And the backward child can be handled more efficiently too.

"We also don't require all our children to develop the same abilities or skills. We don't insist upon a certain set of courses. I don't suppose we have a single child who has had a 'secondary school education,' whatever that means. But they've all developed as rapidly as advisable, and they're well educated in many useful respects. By the same token we don't waste time in teaching the unteachable. The fixed education represented by a diploma is a bit of conspicuous waste which has no place in Walden Two. We don't attach an economic or honorific value to education. It has its own value or none at all.

"Since our children remain happy, energetic, and curious, we don't need to teach 'subjects' at all. We teach only the techniques of learning and thinking. As for geography, literature, the sciences — we give our children opportunity and guidance, and they learn them for themselves. In that way we dispense with half the teachers required under the old system, and the education is incomparably better. Our children aren't neglected, but they're seldom, if ever, taught anything.

"Education in Walden Two is part of the life of the community. We don't need to resort to trumped-up life experiences. Our children begin to work at a very early age. It's no hardship; it's accepted as readily as sport or play. And a good share of our education goes on in workshops, laboratories, and fields. It's part of the Walden Two Code to encourage children in all the arts and crafts. We're glad to spend time in instructing them, for we know it's important for the future of Walden Two and our own security."

"What about higher education?" I said.

"We aren't equipped for professional training, of course," said Frazier. "Those who want to go on to graduate study in a university are given special preparation. Entrance requirements are always tyrannical, though perhaps inevitable in a mass-production system. So far, we've been able to find graduate schools that will take our young people as special students, and as they continue to make excellent records, we expect fewer difficulties. If worse comes to worst, we shall organize as a college and get ourselves accredited. But can you imagine the stupid changes we should have to make?" Frazier snorted with impatience. "Oh, well. Tongue in cheek. Tongue in cheek."

"Don't you mean 'chin up?' " I asked.

"We'd have to set up a 'curriculum,' require a 'C average,' a 'foreign language,' 'so many years of residence,' and so on, and so on. It would be most amusing. No, 'tongue in cheek' was what I meant."

"Your people don't go to college, then?"

"We have no more reason to distinguish between college and high school than between high school and grade school. What are these distinctions, anyway, once you have separated education from the administration of education? Are there any natural breaks in a child's development? Many of our children naturally study more and more advanced material as they grow older. We help them in every way short of teaching them. We give them new techniques of acquiring knowledge and thinking. In spite of the beliefs of most educators, our children are taught to think. We give them an excellent survey of the methods and techniques in thinking, taken from logic, statistics, scientific method, psychology, and mathematics. That's all the 'college education' they need. They get the rest for themselves in our libraries and laboratories."

"But what about libraries and laboratories, though?" I said. "What can you actually provide in that line?"

"As to a library, we pride ourselves on having the best books, if not the most. Have you ever spent much time in a large college library? What trash the librarian has saved up in order to report a million volumes in the college catalogue! Bound pamphlets, old journals, ancient junk that even the shoddiest secondhand bookstore would clear from its shelves — all saved on the flimsy pretext that some day someone will want to study the 'history of a field.' Here we have the heart of a great library — not much to please the scholar or specialist, perhaps, but enough to interest the intelligent reader for life. Two or three thousand volumes will do it."

Frazier challenged me with a stare, but I did not wish to fight on such difficult terrain.

"The secret is this," he continued. "We subtract from our shelves as often as we add to them. The result is a collection that never misses fire. We all get something vital every time we take a book from the shelves. If any one wants to follow a special interest we arrange for loans. If anyone wants to browse, we have half a barnful of discarded volumes.

"Our laboratories are good because they are real. Our workshops are really small engineering laboratories, and anyone with a genuine bent can go farther in them than the college student. We teach anatomy in the slaughterhouse, botany in the field, genetics in

the dairy and poultry house, chemistry in the medical building and in the kitchen and dairy laboratory. What more can you ask?"

"And all this is just for the fun of it? You don't feel that some disciplined study is necessary?" said Castle.

"What for?" asked Frazier in unsuccessfully pretended surprise.

"To provide techniques and abilities which will be valuable later," said Castle. "For example, the study of a language."

"Why 'later?' Why not acquire a language when it's valuable? We acquire our own tongue that way! Of course, you're thinking of an educational process which comes to a dead stop sometime around the middle of June in one's last year in college. In Walden Two education goes on forever. It's part of our culture. We can acquire a technique whenever we need it.

"As to languages," Frazier continued, "you must know that even in our largest universities a language department considers itself very well off if two or three students at any one time approach fluency. We can do better than that. A member of Walden Two who once lived in France has interested several of our members, from ten to fifty years old, in the language. You may run into them during your stay. I hear them buzzing around the dining room every now and then, and they add a pleasantly cosmopolitan touch. And I'm told they're developing a good feeling for the French language and French literature. They'll never get any grades or credits, but they're getting French. Is there really any choice? Either French is worth learning, at the time you learn it, or it's not. And let's be sensible.

"I'm still skeptical," said Castle. "Of course, I'm still at a disadvantage in arguing against an accomplished fact." Frazier nodded his head violently. "But not everything has been accomplished," Castle went on. "Your pleasant schoolrooms, your industrious and contented children — these we must accept. But it would take us a long time to find out how well-educated your children really are, according to our standards." Frazier made a move to speak, but Castle hurried on. "I'll admit these standards won't tell us everything. We couldn't ask your children to take our examinations, because they haven't been learning the same things, even in such a field as French. Your students would probably do no better on a second-year French examination than the average Parisian. I'll admit that, and I confess with all the humility I can muster that the kind of learning you've described is the better — if a comparison is possible. It's the ideal which every college teacher glimpses now and then when he looks up from the dance of death in which he has been caught. But I can't swallow the system you've described because I

don't see what keeps the motors running. Why do your children learn anything at all? What are your substitutes for our standard motives?"

"Your 'standard motives' — exactly," said Frazier. "And there's the rub. An educational institution spends most of its time, not in presenting facts or imparting techniques of learning, but in trying to make its students learn. It has to create spurious needs. Have you ever stopped to analyze them? What are the 'standard motives,' Mr. Castle?"

"I must admit they're not very attractive," said Castle. "I suppose they consist of fear of one's family in the event of low grades or expulsion, the award of grades and honors, the snob value of a cap and gown, the cash value of a diploma."

"Very good, Mr. Castle," said Frazier. "You're an honest man. And now to answer your question — our substitute is simply the absence of these devices. We have had to uncover the worthwhile and truly productive motives — the motives which inspire creative work in science and art outside the academies. No one asks how to motivate a baby. A baby naturally explores everything it can get at, unless restraining forces have already been at work. And this tendency doesn't die out, it's wiped out.

"We made a survey of the motives of the unhampered child and found more than we could use. Our engineering job was to preserve them by fortifying the child against discouragement. We introduce discouragement as carefully as we introduce any other emotional situation, beginning at about six months. Some of the toys in our air-conditioned cubicles are designed to build perseverance. A bit of a tune from a music box, or a pattern of flashing lights, is arranged to follow an appropriate response — say, pulling on a ring. Later the ring must be pulled twice, later still three or five or ten times. It's possible to build up fantastically perservative behavior without encountering frustration or rage. It may not surprise you to learn that some of our experiments miscarried; the resistance to discouragement became almost stupid or pathological. One takes some risks in work of this sort, of course. Fortunately, we were able to reverse the process and restore the children to a satisfactory level.

"Building a tolerance for discouraging events proved to be all we needed," Frazier continued. "The motives in education, Mr. Castle, are the motives in all human behavior. Education should be only life itself. We don't need to create motives. We avoid the spurious academic needs you've just listed so frankly, and also the escape from threat so widely used in our civil institutions. We appeal to the curiosity which is characteristic of the unrestrained child, as well as the alert and inquiring adult. We appeal to that drive to

control the environment which makes a baby continue to crumple a piece of noisy paper and the scientist continue to press forward with his predictive analyses of nature. We don't need to motivate anyone by creating spurious needs."

"I've known a few men with the kind of motivation you mean," I said.

"The contemporary culture produces a few by accident," said Frazier quickly, *"just as it produces a few brave or happy men."*

"But I've never understood them," I said rather faintly.

"Why should you, any more than unhappy people can understand the happy ones?"

"But isn't there a real need for the spurious satisfactions?" I said. *"Little signs of personal success, money — personal domination, too, if you like. Most of what I do, I do to avoid undesirable consequences, to evade unpleasantnesses, or to reject or attack forces which interfere with my freedom."*

"All the unhappy motives," said Frazier.

"Unhappy, perhaps, but powerful, I think the very thing which seems most unpromising in your system is its happiness. Your people are going to be too happy, too successful. But why won't they just go to sleep? Can we expect real achievements from them? Haven't the great men of history been essentially unhappy or maladjusted or neurotic?"

"I have little interest in conclusions drawn from history," said Frazier, *but if you must play that game, I'll play it too. For every genius you cite whose greatness seems to have sprung from a neurosis, I will undertake to cite similar acts of greatness without neurosis. Turn it around and I'll agree. A man with a touch of genius will be so likely to attack existing institutions that he'll be called unbalanced or neurotic. The only geniuses produced by the chaos of society are those who do something about it."* Frazier paused, and I wondered if he were thinking of himself. *"Chaos breeds geniuses. It offers a man something to be a genius about. But here, we have better things to do."*

"But what about the cases where unhappiness has led to artistic or scientific achievement?" I asked.

"Oh, I daresay a few first-rate sonnets would have remained unwritten had the lady yielded," said Frazier. *"But not so many, at that. Not many works of art can be traced to the lack of satisfaction of the basic needs. It's not plain sex that gives rise to art, but personal relations which are social or cultural rather than biological. Art deals with something less obvious than the satisfaction to be*

found in a square meal." Frazier laughed explosively, as if he had perhaps said more than he intended.

"We shall never produce so satisfying a world that there will be no place for art," he continued. "On the contrary, Walden Two has demonstrated very nicely that as soon as the simple necessities of life are obtained with little effort, there's an enormous welling up of artistic interest. And least of all do we need to fear that simple satisfactions will detract from the scientific conquest of the world. What scientist worth the name is engaged, as scientist, in the satisfaction of his own basic needs? He may be thinking of the basic needs of others, but his own motives are clearly cultural. There can be no doubt of the survival value of the inquiring spirit — of curiosity, of exploration, of the need to dominate media, of the urge to control the forces of nature. The world will never be wholly known, and man can't help trying to know more and more of it."

The topic seemed to have grown too vague to stimulate further discussion, but Castle soon offered a substitute.

"I'm torn between two questions which seem incompatible yet equally pressing," he said. "What do you do about differences among your children in intellect and talent? And what do you do to avoid producing a lot of completely standardized young people? Which question should I ask, and what's your answer?"

"They're both good questions," said Frazier, "and quite compatible." I made a move to speak and Frazier said, "I see that Mr. Burris wants to help with the answers."

"My guess is," I said, "that differences are due to environmental and cultural factors and that Mr. Frazier has no great problem to solve. Give all your children the excellent care we have just been witnessing and your differences will be negligible."

"No, you're wrong, Burris," said Frazier. "That's one question we have answered to our satisfaction. Our ten-year-olds have all had the same environment since birth, but the range of their IQ's is almost as great as in the population at large. This seems to be true of other abilities and skills as well."

"And of physical prowess, of course," said Castle.

"Why do you say 'of course?' " said Frazier, with marked interest.

"Why, I suppose because physical differences are generally acknowledged.

"All differences are physical, my dear Mr. Castle. We think with our bodies, too. You might have replied that differences in prowess have always been obvious and impossible to conceal, while other

differences have customarily been disguised for the sake of prestige and family pride. We accept our gross physical limitations without protest and are reasonably happy in spite of them, but we may spend a lifetime trying to live up to a wholly false conception of our powers in another field, and suffer the pain of a lingering failure. Here we accept ourselves as we are."

"Aren't the untalented going to be unhappy?"

"But we don't go in for personal rivalry; individuals are seldom compared. We never develop a taste much beyond a talent. Our parents have little reason to misrepresent their children's abilities to themselves or others. It's easy for our children to accept their limitations — exactly as they have always accepted the gross differences which Mr. Castle called physical prowess. At the same time our gifted children aren't held back by organized mediocrity. We don't throw our geniuses off balance. The brilliant but unstable type is unfamiliar here. Genius can express itself."

BIBLIOGRAPHY

General References

Berneri, Marie Louise. *Journey Through Utopia.* London: Routledge and Kegan Paul, 1950.

Brameld, Theodore. *Toward A Reconstructed Philosophy of Education.* New York: The Dryden Press, Inc., 1956.

Buber, Martin. *Paths in Utopia.* Trans. R. F. C. Hull. London: Routledge and Kegan Paul, Ltd., 1949.

Davis, Jerome. *Contemporary Social Movements.* New York: The Century Co., 1930.

Hertzler, J. O. *History of Utopian Thought.* New York: The Macmillan Co., 1923.

Infield, Henrik F. *Utopias and Experiment.* New York: Frederick A. Praeger, 1955.

Kaufman, M. *Utopias; or Schemes of Social Improvement, from Sir Thomas More to Karl Marx.* London: C. Kegan Paul and Co., 1879.

Mannheim, Karl. *Ideology and Utopia.* New York: Harcourt and Co., 1936.

Mannin, Ethel. *Bread and Roses.* London: Macdonald and Co., Ltd., 1944.

Masso, Gildo. *Education in Utopias.* New York: Teachers College, Columbia University, 1927.

Mumford, Lewis. *The Story of Utopias.* New York: Boni and Liveright, 1922.

Negley, Glenn and J. Max Patrick. *The Quest for Utopia.* New York: Henry Schuman, 1952.

Russell, Frances Theresa. *Touring Utopia*. New York: Dial Press, Inc., 1932.

Westmeyer, Russell E. *Modern Economic and Social Systems*. New York: Farrar and Tinehart, Inc., 1940.

Whitman, John Pratt. *Utopia Dawns*. Boston: Utopia Publishing Co., 1934.

Chapter One

Books and Pamphlets

Crossman, R.H.S. *Plato Today*. London: George Allen and Unwin, Ltd., 1937.

Cushman, Robert E. *Therapeia*. Chapel Hill: University of North Carolina Press, 1958.

Hoerber, Robert George. *The Theme of Plato's Republic*. St. Louis: Eden Publishing House, 1944.

Joseph, H. W. B. *Knowledge and the Good in Plato's Republic*. London: Oxford University Press, 1948.

Livingstone, Sir Richard. *Plato and Modern Education*. Cambridge University Press, 1944.

Lodge, R. C. *Plato's Theory of Ethics*. New York: Harcourt, Brace and Co., 1920.

Murphy, N. R. *The Interpretation of Plato's Republic*. Oxford: Clarendon Press, 1951.

Nettleship, R. L. *The Theory of Education in Plato's Republic*. London: Oxford University Press, 1935.

Plato. *Republic*. Trans. Francis MacDonald Cornford. New York: Oxford University Press, 1945.

Popper, Karl R. *The Open Society and Its Enemies*. Princeton: Princeton University Press, 1950.

Shorey, Paul. *What Plato Said*. Chicago: University of Chicago Press, 1933.

Taylor, A. E. *Plato; The Man and His Work.* New York: Meridian Books, 1957.

Wild, John. *Plato's Modern Enemies and the Theory of Natural Law.* Chicago: University of Chicago Press, 1959.

Winspear, Alban Dewes. *The Genesis of Plato's Thought.* New York: S. A. Russell, 1956.

Periodicals

Burrell, P. S. "The Plot of Plato's Republic," *Mind,* New Series, 97:56-82, January, 1916.

Duncan, Sir Patrick. "Socrates and Plato," *Philosophy,* 15:339-362, October, 1940.

Field, G. C. "Great Thinkers – Plato," *Philosophy,* 9:282-292, July, 1934.

Stewart, J. A. "Socratès and Plato," *Mind,* New Series, 104:393-406, October, 1917.

Chapter Two

Books and Pamphlets

Ames, Russell. *Citizen Thomas More; and His Utopia.* Princeton: Princeton University Press, 1949.

Berneri, Marie Louise. *Journey Through Utopia.* London: Routledge and Kegan Paul, Ltd., 1950.

Bremond, Henri. *Sir Thomas More.* London: Duckworth and Co., 1904.

Chambers, R. W. *The Place of Saint Thomas More in English Literature and History.* London: Longmans, Green and Co., 1937.

Cecil, Algernon. *A Portrait of Thomas More; Scholar, Statesman, Saint.* London: Eyre and Spottiswoode, 1937.

de B. Gibbins, H. *English Social Reformers.* London: Methuen and Co., 1892.

Donner, H. W. *Introduction to Utopia.* London: Sidgwick and Jackson, Ltd., 1945.

Dudok, Gerard. *Sir Thomas More and His Utopia.* Amsterdam: H. J. Paris, 1924.

Kautsky, Karl. *Thomas More and His Utopia* New York: International Publishers, 1937.

Masso, Gildo. *Education in Utopias.* New York: Teachers College, Columbia University, 1927.

More, Thomas. *Utopia.* In *Ideal Empires and Republics.* London: M. Walter Dunne, 1901.

Reynolds, E. E. *Saint Thomas More.* London: Burns Oates, 1953.

Surtz, Edward. *The Praise of Pleasure; Philosophy, Education. and Communism in More's Utopia.* Cambridge: Harvard University Press, 1957.

_____. *The Praise of Wisdom.* Chicago: Loyola University Press, 1957.

Whitman, John Pratt. *Utopia Dawns.* Boston: Utopia Publishing Co., 1934.

Periodicals

Adams, Robert P. "The Philosophic Unity of More's Utopia," *Studies in Philology,* 38:45-65, January, 1941.

Chambers, R. W. "The Saga and the Myth of Sir Thomas More," *Proceedings of the British Academy.* (London: Oxford University Press, 1926), 179-225.

Goodier, Alban. "The World Vision of St. Thomas More," *The Month,* 172:109-117, August, 1938.

Parks, George B. "More's Utopia and Geography," *The Journal of English and Germanic Philology,* 37:224-236, April, 1938.

Sowards, J. K. "Some Factors in the Re-evaluation of Thomas More's Utopia," *The Northwest Missouri State College Studies,* 16:31-58, June, 1952.

Chapter Three

Books and Pamphlets

Bonansea, Bernardino M. *The Theory of Knowledge of Tommaso Campanella.* Washington: The Catholic University of America Press, 1954.

Campanella, Thomas. *City of the Sun.* In *Ideal Empires and Republics.* London: M. Walter Dunne, 1901.

_____. *The Defense of Galileo.* Northampton: Smith College Studies in History, 22, April-July, 1937.

Grillo, Francesco. *Tommaso Campanella.* New York: S. F. Vanni, 1954.

Hertzler, J. O. *The History of Utopian Thought.* New York: The Macmillan Company, 1923.

Negley, Glenn and J. Max Patrick. *The Quest for Utopia.* New York: Henry Schuman, 1952.

Whitman, John Pratt. *Utopia Dawns.* Boston: Utopia Publishing Company, 1934.

Periodicals

Blodgett, Eleanor Dickinson. "Bacon's New Atlantis and Campanella's Civitas Solis: A Study in Relationships," *Publications of the Modern Language Association,* 46:763-780, September, 1931.

Chapter Four

Books and Pamphlets

Andreae, Johann Valentin. *Christianopolis.* Trans. Felix Emil Held. New York: Oxford University Press, 1916.

Berneri, Marie Louise. *Journey Through Utopia.* London: Routledge and Kegan Paul, Ltd., 1950.

Morgan, Arthur E. *Nowhere was Somewhere.* Chapel Hill: University of North Carolina Press, 1946.

Negley, Glenn and J. Max Patrick. *The Quest for Utopia.* New York: Henry Schuman Company, 1952.

Whitman, John Pratt. *Utopia Dawns.* Boston: Utopia Publishing Company, 1934.

Chapter Five

Books and Pamphlets

de Sola Pool, D. *Hebrew Learning Among the Puritans of New England Prior to 1700.* Publication of the American Jewish Historical Society, No. 20, 1911.

Gott, Samuel. *Nova Solyma.* Trans. Walter Begley. New York: Charles Scribner's Sons, 1902.

Periodicals

Collins, J. Churton. "Miltonic Myths and Their Authors," *The National Review,* July, 1904, 768-785.

Jones, Stephen K. "The Authorship of 'Nova Solyma'," *The Library,* Third Series, 1:225-238, July, 1910.

Patrick, J. Max. "Puritanism and Poetry: Samuel Gott," *University of Toronto Quarterly,* January, 1939, 211-226.

Chapter Six

Books and Pamphlets

Aiton, John. *Mr. Owen's Objections to Christianity, and New View of Society, and Education, Refuted by A Plain Statement of Facts, with a Hint to Archibald Hamilton, Esq., of Dalziel.* Edinburgh: James Robertson and Co., 1824.

Bestor, Arthur E., Jr. *Backwoods Utopias; The Sectarian and Owenite Phases of Communitarian Socialism in America 1663-1829.* Philadelphia: University of Pennsylvania Press, 1950.

Brown, John. *Remarks on the Plans and Publications of Robert Owen of New Lanark.* Edinburgh: Ogle, Allardice, and Thomson, 1817.

Cole, Margaret. *Robert Owen of New Lanark.* New York: Oxford University Press, 1953.

Davies, R. E. *The Life of Robert Owen.* London: Robert Sutton, 1907.

Fisher, W. L. *An Examination of the New System of Society by Robert Owen, Showing Its Insufficiency to Reform Mankind with Observations on the Operation of the Principle of Virtue in the Mind of Man.* Philadelphia: John Mortimer, 1826.

Harvey, Rowland Hill. *Robert Owen, Social Idealist.* Berkeley: University of California Press, 1949.

Jones, Lloyd. *The Life, Times, and Labors of Robert Owen.* New York: George Allen and Unwin, Ltd., 1800.

Owen, Robert. *The Life of Robert Owen.* London: G. Bell and Sons, Ltd., 1920.

_____. *A New View of Society.* London: J. M. Dent and Sons, Ltd., 1927.

_____. *New World Order.* London: R. Taylor, 1836.

Podmore, Frank. *Robert Owen.* London: Hutchinson and Co., 1906.

Periodicals

Gould, Kenneth M. "Robert Owen: Backwater of History?" *The American Scholar,* 7:153-170, Spring, 1938.

Janes, George Milton. "Robert Owen — Social Dreamer," *The Quarterly Journal,* 2:17-24, October, 1920.

Chapter Seven

Books and Pamphlets

Butler, Samuel. *Erewhon.* New York: E. P. Dutton and Company, 1917.

_____ . *Erewhon Revisited.* New York: E. P. Dutton and Company, 1910.

_____ . *Life and Habit.* London: A. C. Fifield, 1916.

_____ . *Note-Books of Samuel Butler.* Edited by H. F. Jones. New York: M. Kennerley, 1913.

Cannan, Gilbert. *Samuel Butler, A Critical Study.* London: Martin Secker, 1915.

Cole, G. D. H. *Samuel Butler.* London: Longmans, Green and Company, 1952.

Furbank, P. N. *Samuel Butler.* Cambridge: University Press, 1948.

Harris, John F. *Samuel Butler: Author of Erewhon; The Man and His Work.* London: Grant Richards, Ltd., 1916.

Joad, C. E. M. *Samuel Butler.* London: Leonard Parsons, 1924.

Muggeridge, Malcolm. *The Earnest Atheist, A Study of Samuel Butler.* London: Eyre and Spottiswoode, 1936.

Periodicals

Cavenaugh, F. A. "Samuel Butler and Education," *The Monist,* 32:307-313, April, 1922.

More, Paul Elmer. "Samuel Butler of Erewhon," *The Unpartizan Review,* 15:20-42, January-March, 1921.

Stanley, Carleton W. "The Author of Erewhon," *Queens Quarterly,* 29:115-137, October-December, 1921.

Yeats, John Butler. "Recollections of Samuel Butler," *The Seven Arts,* August, 1917, 493-501.

Chapter Eight

Books and Pamphlets

Aaron, Daniel. *Men of Good Hope.* New York: Oxford University Press, 1951.

Bellamy, Edward. *Looking Backward.* New York: Harper and Bros., 1959.

_____. *The Religion of Solidarity.* Yellow Springs: Antioch Bookplate Company, 1940.

Berneri, Marie Louise. *Journey Through Utopia.* London: Routledge and Kegan Paul, Ltd., 1950.

Michaelis, Richard. *Looking Further Forward.* New York: Rand, McNally and Company, 1890.

Morgan, Arthur E. *Edward Bellamy.* New York: Columbia University Press, 1944.

_____. *The Philosophy of Edward Bellamy.* New York: King's Crown Press, 1945.

_____. *Plagiarism in Utopia.* Michigan: Edwards Brothers, 1944.

Parrington, Vernon Louis. *American Dreams.* Providence: Brown University Press, 1947.

Schindler, Solomon. *Young West.* Boston: Avena Publishing Company, 1894.

Seager, Allan. *They Worked for a Better World.* New York: The Macmillan Company, 1939.

Periodicals

Franklin, John Hope.   "Edward Bellamy and the Nationalist Movement," *The New England Quarterly,* The University Press, Orono, Maine, December, 1938, 739-772.

Greer, Richard A. "Edward Bellamy, An American Utopian," *The Historian,* University of New Mexico (Autumn, 1941), 103-115.

Madison, Charles A. "Edward Bellamy, Social Dreamer," *The New England Quarterly,* The University Press, Orono, Maine, September, 1942, 444-466.

Sadler, Elizabeth. "One Book's Influence — Edward Bellamy's 'Looking Backward'," *The New England Quarterly,* The University Press, Orono, Maine, December, 1944, 530-555.

Shurter, Robert L. "The Literary Work of Edward Bellamy," *American Literature,* Duke University Press, Durham, North Carolina, November, 1933, 229-234.

_____. "The Writing of Looking Backward," *The South Atlantic Quarterly,* Duke University Press, Durham, North Carolina, July, 1939, 255-261.

Chapter Nine

Books and Pamphlets

Barker, Arthur. *William Morris.* London: Paul Bloomfield, Ltd., 1934.

Clutton-Brock, A. *William Morris: His Work and Influence.* London: Williams and Norgate, 1914.

Compton-Rickett, Arthur *William Morris: A Study in Personality.* London: Herbert Jenkins, Ltd., 1913.

Eshleman, Lloyd Wendell. *A Victorian Rebel: The Life of William Morris,* New York: Charles Scribner's Sons, 1940.

Glasier, J. Bruce. *William Morris: and the Early Days of the Socialist Movement.* London: Longmans, Green, and Company, 1921.

Grennan, Margaret R. *William Morris, Medievalist and Revolutionary.* New York: King's Crown Press, 1945.

Morris, William. *News from Nowhere.* London: Reeves and Turner, 1891.

_____. *On Art and Socialism.* London: John Lehmann, 1947.

Noyes, Alfred. *William Morris.* London: Macmillan Company, 1908.

Shaw, George Bernard. *William Morris, As I Knew Him.* New York: Dodd, Mead, and Company, 1936.

von Helmholtz-Phelan, Anna A. *The Social Philosophy of William Morris.* Durham: Duke University Press, 1927.

Periodicals

Arnot, R. Page. "William Morris versus The Morris Myth," *The Labour Monthly,* 16:178-184, March, 1934.

Chapter Ten

Books and Pamphlets

Cram, Ralph Adams. *Convictions and Controversies.* Boston: Marshall Jones Company, 1935.

_____. *The Nemesis of Mediocrity.* Boston: Marshall Jones Company, 1917.

_____. *The Sins of the Fathers.* Boston: Marshall Jones Company, 1918.

_____. *Towards the Great Peace.* Boston: Marshall Jones Company, 1922.

_____. *Walled Towns.* Boston: Marshall Jones Company, 1919.

Periodicals

Cram, Ralph Adams. "Art and Contemporary Society," *The Barnwell Bulletin,* 8:17-29, February, 1931.

_____. "The Limitations of Democracy," *The Rice Institute Pamphlet,* 17:175-199, July, 1930.

_____. "The Way of Youth; A Chapter from an Autobiography," *The American Review,* 5:513-530, October, 1935.

Chapter Eleven

Books and Pamphlets

Beresford, J. D. *H. G. Wells.* New York: Henry Holt and Company, 1915.

Braybrooke, Patrick. *Some Aspects of H. G. Wells.* London: C. W. Daniel Company, 1928.

Brooks, Van Wyck. *The World of H. G. Wells.* New York: Mitchell Kinnerley, 1915.

Brown, Ivor. *H. G. Wells.* New York: Henry Holt and Company, 1924.

Chappell, Fred A. *Bibliography of H. G. Wells.* Chicago: Covici-McGee Company, 1924.

Doughty, F. H. *H. G. Wells; Educationist?* New York: George H. Doran Company, 1927.

Nicholson, Norman. *H. G. Wells.* London: A. Barker, 1950.

Wells, H. G. *The Discovery of the Future.* London: Jonathan Cape, Ltd., 1913.

_____. *Joan and Peter.* New York: The Macmillan Company, 1918.

_____. *Mankind in the Making.* New York: Charles Scribner's Sons, 1918.

_____. *A Modern Utopia.* London: Chapman and Hall, Ltd., 1905.

_____. *The New World Order.* New York: Alfred A. Knopf, 1940.

_____. *The Open Conspiracy.* London: Victor Gollancz, 1928.

_____. *The Salvaging of Civilization.* New York: The Macmillan Company, 1921.

_____. *The Undying Fire.* New York: The Macmillan Company, 1919.

_____. *What Are We to Do with Our Lives.* New York: Doubleday, Doran and Company, 1931.

Periodicals

Collis, J. S. "H. G. Wells – A New Scrutiny," *The Bermondsey Book,* 5:56-59, December, January, February, 1927-1828.

Davis, Ada E. "H. G. Wells on Education," *Education,* 46:72-95, October, 1925.

Davis, Elmer. "Notes on the Failure of a Mission," *The Saturday Review of Literature,* 29:6-8, August 31, 1946.

Fadiman, Clifton. "The Passing of a Prophet," *The Saturday Review of Literature,* 29:3-6, August 31, 1946.

Kaempffert, Waldemar. "Evangelist of Utopia," *The Saturday Review of Literature,* 29:8-9, August 31, 1946.

Lloyd, D. B. "The World and Mr. Wells," *The Quarterly Review,* 259:49-61, July, 1932.

Chapter Twelve

Books and Pamphlets

Henderson, Alexander. *Aldous Huxley.* London: Chatto and Windus, 1935.

Huxley, Aldous. *Brave New World.* New York: Bantam Books, 1932.

_____. *Brave New World Revisited.* New York: Harper and Bros., 1958.

_____. *Do What You Will.* New York: Doubleday, Doran and Company, 1928.

_____. *Ends and Means.* New York: Harper and Bros., 1937.

_____ *Jesting Pilate.* New York: George H. Doran Company, 1926.

_____. *The Perennial Philosophy.* London: Chatto and Windus, 1946.

_____. *Proper Studies.* New York: Doubleday, Doran and Company, 1928.

_____. *Tomorrow and Tomorrow and Tomorrow; and Other Essays.* New York: Harper and Bros., 1952.

Orwell, George *1984.* New York: Harcourt, Brace and Company, 1949.

Periodicals

Estrich, Helen Watts. "Jesting Pilate Tells the Answer," *Sewanee Review,* 47:63-81, January-March, 1939.

Glicksberg, C. I. "The Intellectual Pilgrimage of Aldous Huxley," *The Dalhousie Review,* 19:165-178, July, 1939.

Hyde, Lawrence. "Aldous Huxley: 'Life Worshipper'," *The New Adelphi,* 3:90-102, December-February, 1930.

Kooistra, J. "Aldous Huxley," *English Studies,* 13:161-175, October, 1931.

Thompson, Sydney. "Aldous Huxley," *Humberside* (Hull, England), 3:247-259, October, 1930.

Chapter Thirteen

Books and Pamphlets

Ferster, C. B. and B. F. Skinner. *Schedules of Reinforcement.* New York: Appleton-Century-Crofts, Inc. 1957.

Orwell, George *1984.* New York: Harcourt, Brace and Company, 1949.

Skinner, B. F. *Cumulative Record.* New York: Appleton-Century-Crofts, Inc., 1959.

_____. *Science and Human Behavior.* New York: The Macmillan Company, 1953.

_____. *Verbal Behavior.* New York: Appleton-Century-Crofts, Inc., 1957.

_____. *Walden Two,* New York: The Macmillan Company, 1948.

Periodicals

Hamburg, Carl H. "Skinner's 'scientific' ethics of survival," *Tulane
    Studies in Philosophy* (New Orleans, Louisiana), 4:49-60,
    1955.

BIOGRAPHICAL NOTES

PLATO (428-347 B. C.)

Plato· was born in Athens, Greece, the son of an aristocratic family. He received the typical education for well-to-do children, and early in life began the study of philosophy. At the age of twenty he became a disciple of Socrates, to whom he remained devoted until Socrates' death seven years later. Plato afterwards founded and directed a school known as the "Academy." This school was to be a training place for future political leaders who were to restore decent government to the cities of Greece. Plato lived out his last years in seclusion at the Academy, where many honors were bestowed upon him. He died there at the age of eighty-one.

THOMAS MORE (1478-1535)

Thomas More was born in London, England. He attended St. Anthony's School on Threadneedle Street, and at thirteen was placed in the household of Cardinal Morton, Archbishop of Canterbury. He attended Oxford University and New Inn. He distinguished himself in professional studies and acquired great facility in Greek, from which he published translations. He entered the King's service and served in several ambassadorial posts, later to become chancellor of the duchy of Lancaster, under Henry VIII. When he objected on religious grounds to the King's effort to divorce his present wife so that he could marry Anne Boleyn, More was forced to resign from government office and was later imprisoned in the Tower of London. He was hanged on the scaffold in 1535, and canonized as a saint by the Roman Catholic Church in 1935.

THOMAS CAMPANELLA (1568-1639)

Campanella was born at Stilo in the province of Calabria, Italy. At thirteen, he was already an accomplished writer of verse and prose, and at fourteen he joined the Dominican Order. He attended various institutions, including the University of Padua. In 1603, he was charged with attempting to overthrow the Spanish government in Naples and sentenced to twenty-seven years of imprisonment. During his confinement, he wrote many philosophical and political works. With the Pope's protection he was released in 1629, and died in Paris ten years later.

JOHANN VALENTIN ANDREAE (1586-1654)

Johann Valentin Andreae was born at Herrenberg, Germany. He attended the University at Tubingen, where he published several pedagogical works. He traveled widely in Europe and absorbed the spirit of the Renaissance. Andreae was also influenced by the Protestant Reformation and entered the Lutheran ministry. He later served in important posts in Europe where he made significant educational and social changes. He died in Adelburg, Germany.

SAMUEL GOTT (1613-1671)

Samuel Gott was born in London, four years after the birth of John Milton. His father, an ironmonger reputed to be a man of some means, sent him to Merchant Taylor's School and to Saint Catherine's College, Cambridge, where *Nova Solyma* is believed to have been created. In March 1633 he was admitted to the Society of Gray's Inn. Gott was called to the bar in 1640, but probably did not practice. After his father's death in 1642, he married and lived quietly on a country estate in Battle, England. He returned to London only for a short residence, during which time he was elected an "Ancient." He was buried in Battle, England.

ROBERT OWEN (1771-1858)

Robert Owen was born at Newtown, Montgomeryshire, England. When he was only twenty-six, Owen and some others purchased the cotton mills in New Lanark, Scotland, which they called the New Lanark Twist Company, While at New Lanark, Owen fought continuously for various labor and social reforms, and traveled widely preaching his humanitarian doctrines. In 1828, he severed his connections with the mills, and founded an experimental community in the United States at Harmony, Indiana, called New Harmony. This program failed, and Owen then turned his attention to organizing a trade union in Great Britain which would encompass all trade unions. This, also, was a failure. He died at his birthplace in Newtown.

SAMUEL BUTLER (1835-1902)

Samuel Butler was born near Bingham, Nottinghamshire, England. Many of the scenes of his childhood can be found in *The Way of All Flesh.* Butler went to St. John's College, Cambridge. He left England in 1859 to raise sheep in New Zealand. The New Zealand countryside formed the background for *Erewhon,* and there is now a place in New Zealand by that name, after Butler's book. In 1864, he sold his sheep run and returned to England. For the next thirty-eight years, until his death, his time was spent in painting, writing, and traveling.

EDWARD BELLAMY (1850-1898)

Edward Bellamy was born in Chicopee Falls, Massachusetts. His father was a minister. He spent one year at Union College, studied law, and was later admitted to the bar in Hampden County, Massachusetts. He took up journalism and was later associated with the New York Evening Post, the Springfield Union, and the Berkshire Courier. He helped to found the Springfield Daily News and the New Nation. His greatest work, *Looking Backward,* sold over one million copies. He lectured, traveled, and wrote on behalf of "Nationalism," one of the themes of his book, until his death.

WILLIAM MORRIS (1834-1896)

William Morris was born at Walthamston, England. He was the eldest son of a well-to-do family. Morris attended Oxford, where he studied architecture and wrote poetry. He later became famous both as a poet and a designer. In his forty-seventh year he became a socialist, and from then on devoted much of his time to promoting socialist ideas through lectures and writings. Morris died at his home in Kelmscott, England.

RALPH ADAMS CRAM (1863-1942)

Ralph Adams Cram was born at Hampton Falls, New Hampshire. He began work as an architect when he was twenty-six years of age. He specialized in the construction of ecclesiastical and educational buildings and became one of the leading authorities on Gothic architecture. He was chosen as consulting architect for the Cathedral of St. John the Divine in New York City, and also wrote several books and articles on social and aesthetic subjects.

HERBERT GEORGE WELLS (1866-1946)

H. G. Wells was born at Bromley, London, England. His father was a shopkeeper, and his mother, before marriage, had been a maid. He was educated at Midhurst and the Royal College of Science, London University. He turned to journalism after having been a draper, druggist, and schoolteacher. His total works equal more than one hundred and twenty-six volumes, dealing with a variety of subjects. His *The Outline of History* sold more copies than any other of his works. He was twice married and lived in London and on the Rivera. He died in London.

ALDOUS HUXLEY (1894-1963)

Aldous Huxley was born at Godalmin in Surrey, England. His grandfather was Thomas Henry Huxley, the famous biologist. His father was Leonard Huxley, a writer; and his mother was a niece of Matthew Arnold. His brother, Julian, also became a writer, as well as a scientist. Aldous Huxley was educated at Eton and Oxford, and from 1923 to 1930 wrote novels in Italy and associated with D. H. Lawrence. He lived for many years in southern California.

BURRHUS FREDERICK SKINNER (1904-   )

B. F. Skinner was born in Susquehanna, Pennsylvania. He received an A.B. from Hamilton College, and his M.A. and Ph.D. from Harvard University. He taught at the University of Minnesota and Indiana University, and for a year was a member of the research staff at General Mills, Inc. Professor Skinner is well known for his work with pigeons in developing reinforcement theories, and for his research and writings about teaching machines. In 1942 he received the Howard Crosby Warren Medal Award in Psychology for outstanding work in the field of experimental psychology. Professor Skinner is presently teaching at Harvard.

OTHER UTOPIAN WORKS WHICH DEAL WITH EDUCATION

Bacon, Francis. *The New Atlantis.* 1629.

Berington, Simon. *The Adventures of Guadentio di Lucca.* 1737.

Blatchford, Robert. *The Sorcery Shop.* 1909.

Buckingham, James Silk. *National Evils and Practical Remedies.* 1848.

Bulwer-Lytton, Edward Lytton. *The Coming Race.* 1928.

Cabet, Etienne. *Voyage in Icaria.* 1848.

Chambless, Edgar. *Roadtown.* 1910.

France, Anatole. *The White Stone.* 1910.

Harrington, James. *Oceana.* 1656.

Hertzka, Theodor. *Freeland, A Social Anticipation.* 1889.

Howells, W. D. *A Traveller from Alturia.* 1894.

Hudson, W. H. *A Crystal Age.* 1906.

Kirwan, Thomas. *Reciprocity in the Thirtieth Century.* 1909.

Mantegazza, Paolo. *The Year 3000.* 1897.

Mercier, Louis Sebastien. *Memoirs of the Year 2500.* 1791.

Orwell, George. *1984.* 1949.

Pemberton, Robert. *The Happy Colony.* 1854.

Richmond, Sir William Blake. *Democracy: False or True?* 1920.

Russell, T. Baron. *A Hundred Years Hence.* 1905.

Spense,Thomas. *Spensonia.* 1795.

Sweven, Godfrey. *Limanora, The Island of Progress.* 1903.

Tarbouriech, Ernest. *The City of the Future.* 1902.

Tarde, Gabriel. *Underground Man.* 1905.

Vayrasse d'Alais, Dennis. *The History of the Sevarites.* 1672.